EARTH
HONORING

EARTH
HONORING

THE NEW MALE
SEXUALITY

BY
ROBERT LAWLOR

Park Street Press
ROCHESTER · VERMONT

Park Street Press
One Park Street
Rochester, Vermont 05767

LIBRARY OF CONGRESS CATALOGING-IN-PUBLICATION DATA

Lawlor, Robert.
  Earth honoring : the new male sexuality / by Robert Lawlor.
    p. cm.
  Bibliography: p.
  Includes index.
  ISBN 0-89281-428-4
  1. Men—Sexual behavior.   2. Sex (Psychology)   3. Masculinity (Psychology) I. Title.
HQ28.L39 1989
306.7'088041—dc19

Text design by Sushila Blackman

Printed and bound in the United States

10 9 8 7 6 5 4 3 2 1

Park Street Press is a division of Inner Traditions International, Ltd.

Distributed to the book trade in the United States by American International Distribution Corporation (AIDC)

Distributed to the book trade in Canada by Book Center, Inc., Montreal, Quebec.

This book is dedicated to Fritz Bultman,
artist, teacher, and friend,
who in his work always revealed the
spiritual aspect of human sexuality.

CONTENTS

PART 3 • SEXUALITY AND SOCIETY

I wish to give special thanks to Edward C. Whitmont, Return of the Goddess, *and Morris Berman,* The Reenchantment of the World. *Their extensive research and profound insights provided the foundation for this book. I hope that the direction in which I carried some of our shared premises will be satisfying and of interest to them. I should like to thank Alain Danielou, whose illusionless interpretation of prehistoric and ancient Indian society opens up our imaginal potential for a new sense of the future.*

I would like to personally thank Nadia Weiner and Deirdre O'Connell for their tireless assistance and encouragement and especially Joanna Lambert who gave the research life and meaning.

INTRODUCTION

One glance at the shelves in popular bookstores tells the story. There are dozens of titles about female sexuality: women are offered guidance and explanations galore during this tumultuous and confusing transition of sexual conventions and sexual roles. But on those same shelves only a few titles can be found directed to the problems men face in the wake of the "sexual revolution." With this book, I hope to help correct that imbalance.

I believe the models we are using to reformulate the concept and role of male sexuality in modern society are not derived from a wide enough slice of history (modern psychology is barely a century old). Through modern scholarship we are learning much more about ancient patterns of male/female interrelationships that, I believe, can be enormously useful today when applied to our practical well-being, our spiritual growth, and our sexual delight. As well, these patterns reveal the origins of some of the enormous problems that besiege the modern world.

Our sense of self, society, and spirituality are inseparably linked to our sexuality. This book explores the particular role of male sexuality in the formation of these three vital areas of life. In it I attempt to show how an imbalance in male sexuality is at the core of many contemporary problems, such as: the destruction and exploitation of the environment; continuous war and aggression, crime, rape and terrorism, political corruption; the degeneration of public health, sexually transmitted diseases; the collapse of social institutions, such as marriage and the family; obsessive materialism and industrialism, the vulgarity and meaninglessness of most public entertainment; and the emptiness of most modern religious dogmas, ranging from fundamentalist sentimentality and fanaticism to cold puritanical abstraction. The root source of all these problems can, from a certain point of view, be found in an imbalance of male sexuality.

On the positive side, male sexuality can be credited with a brilliant development of skills, structures, and organizations: vast urban systems of government and economic complexes, extraordinary expertise and innovation in the accumulation of information. All of these qualities, along with the inspiring expansion of humanity's place in the world against the limits of nature can be associated with a force of energy particular to male sexuality. To understand how these powers and problems manifest in our world, and how they begin to change and evolve, the fundamental nature of male sexuality must be reexamined and revised.

This book is not about pop psychology; nor is it a sex manual showing exotic sexual skills to increase the lovemaking expertise of modern men (although some of both are included). It is a book that looks at male sexuality from a broader perspective. This includes a look at how the thought patterns generally associated with masculinity grow out of male sexuality and male physicality. I attempt to examine the role of male sexuality in the formation of society, as contrasted with that of the female, particularly in relation to the tribal Earth-Mother cultures. I also attempt to show how ancient concepts of sexuality helped create a different social order in certain tribal cultures.

It is my belief that positive changes in the seemingly immense problems of human psychology, society, and spirituality all hinge upon an innovative regeneration of our sexuality; this regeneration must begin with a harmonization and cultivation of lifeforce energies within our own bodies and minds. The influence of sexuality on each of the three major components of life—self, society and spirituality—will be treated in separate sections. Each section has an introductory road map providing key definitions, concepts and information to enable the reader to wind easily through a vast landscape of historical viewpoints on male sexuality that are provocative and full of surprises. Several general signposts ought to be mentioned here to make the entire journey easier.

Throughout, the reader is asked to redefine sexuality in a wide, encompassing way: we live in a universe that is completely dependent on polarity. The very energy that constitutes the universe is a high frequency vibration of pure polarization. Light, as well as all electromagnetic vibration, is characterized by an antagonistic/complementary polarity. All energy has this foundation of mutual attraction and repulsion. All movement is along a continuum from one extreme to its opposite: beginning and ending, expansion and contraction, ascent and descent, life and death.[1] The world is driven by two opposite streams of energy in constant intercourse. To and fro, the motion of copulation is the heartbeat of reality. The universe, from the heavens to atoms, is sexual. Men and women, through the ecstatic state of sexual orgasm, stand poised in a harmony of these opposites: it is our deepest contact with the balance of nature and the origins of existence.

Within the last decade this principle of an ever-shifting dynamic polarity has been widely applied to our understanding of the earth's ecology. Homeostasis is the name of the process by which all life sustains itself, by riding the waves of cyclic oscillations. Cycles of sleeping and waking, secretion and cessation, alkalinity and acidity, fertility and dormancy form the basis of all life. The Gaia hypothesis of James Lovelock and other ecobiologists propose that Earth itself is a living, self-regulatory body. This book suggests that humanity honor the Earth's processes by reflecting and maintaining a balance through our sexuality. Earth and Sky are the cosmic symbols of the Universal Female and Male. The Earth is viewed as the primary physical representation of the qualities of the Universal Feminine; the attitudes and actions toward the Feminine are reflected in our attitudes and actions toward the Earth. Hence the title, *Earth-Honoring: The New Male Sexuality*, addresses the relationship between the disturbances in human sexuality and the crisis in the environmental ecology.

Sexuality is the universal mutual attraction and repulsion of opposites. It is a plan, a strategy, upon which the entire universe is built. It is never a question of one polarity being "bad" and the other "good"—we can never say day is "good" and night is "bad"—they form a complementary, alternating whole. As with all polar opposites, one, by contrast, defines the existence of the other. Likewise, Male and Female cannot be considered separately. Nature always tends to balance extreme polarities cyclically but never to equalize them permanently. Daytime becomes longer, more dominant, in Summer but is shorter in Winter. There is always a shifting, balancing and rebalancing of opposites through the natural cycles of time. I explore in this book these alternating cycles in the evolution of the dominant and submissive patterns of male and female sexuality throughout long periods of our history, as well as within our own lives. We shall be dealing with large ideas concerning human sexuality and envisioning some of the deep original causes, rather than the symptoms, of many modern-day crises.

Modern psychological theory commonly stresses the importance and responsibility of the individual for creating and controlling his or her own destiny. Yet we are always and at the same time a collective creature. Our fate as individuals is never separable from the fate of our race, our society, our ancestors, our planet. We shall therefore look at male sexuality in the context of its social as well as its personal impact and implications. Like the polarity of Male and Female, society and individual are in an inseparable relationship.

I·

SEXUALITY AND SELF

ROADMAP: THE CRISIS
IN MALE IDENTITY

Our identity begins with sexual identity. Sex is the primary category of differentiation of the human creature. Such categories as race, nationality, social class, and education then round out the general format of our identity. Psychology represents the aspect of our self-identity that arises from the inner nature of human consciousness.

The history of psychology has been shaped by three major personalities: Sigmund Freud, Carl Jung and Wilhelm Reich. More recently, a fourth factor, ancient Eastern philosophical concepts, has radically altered our understanding of human psychology. As a map for this exploration of the relationship of sexuality and self-identity, I use a summary of the important contribution of each of these four major influences. Each contribution is a new branch extending from the same tree of growth. That growth, through time, can be imaged as a process connecting the timeless division of human nature: Body, Emotion, Mind, Spirit.

The Austrian psychiatrist Sigmund Freud (1856-1939) was the first Western thinker to posit sexuality as the foundation of human psychology and identity. He introduced the idea of the unconscious mind, which he saw as a refuse dump for unwanted, painful, and unacceptable drives and desires. The conscious mind hides this refuse from itself and others, but both individuals and society are burdened, altered, and sometimes disrupted by this unconscious material. Freud's concept of the unconscious mind as the receptacle of repressed, primitive, violent, carnal, and animalistic drives aligned him with the Darwinian view of evolution. These drives, Freud claimed, were solely responsible for dreams, fantasies, neuroses and mental disorders. Ironically, all religion, culture, and art sprang from the same source as neurosis—repressed and sublimated sexuality. Freud opened up an intellectual investigation of the unconscious but denied a spiritual side to human nature, seeing man as merely a victim of heredity, environment, and repressed sexual desires.

The division of humanity into male and female reflects a simple, inescapable and universal fact: the world is based on a plan of *twoness*—everything that exists has its opposite. The characteristics that are universally "masculine" (rationality, intellectualism, perfectionism, aggressiveness, separatism) have their opposite in qualities that are universally "feminine" (intuitiveness, feelings, completeness, receptiveness, connectedness). These universal masculine/feminine states of being are called *archetypal male* and *female*. Throughout this book we will employ this concept of the Absolute Male and Absolute Female. All men and women in the world have different combinations and proportions of the characteristics of these archetypes, but no one person contains the totality of the pure idea. This concept was put forth by a student of Freud, Carl Jung (1865–1951).

According to Jung, since no man or woman purely characterizes the archetypal man or woman, it stands to reason that each man has some feminine traits *(anima)* and each woman has some masculine traits *(animus)*.[1] The animus in a woman allows her the typically masculine capacities for rationality, logic, deliberation, and premeditative control. The anima in a man gives him access to the hidden source of his feelings, his intuition and his ability to give birth to artistic creations. Because each man contains a woman within him and each woman, a man, human love is intensified: each partner is more capable of perceiving his/her own identity within the other.

We have Jung to thank for the opening of Western psychology to the spiritual myths and symbolism of the ancient past. However, Jung did little to relate these broad vistas of human psychology to our physical bodies. This task fell to Wilhelm Reich (1898-1957) who studied with Freud in Vienna. It has been said that Reich found at the roots of existence an energy that, under varied circumstances, becomes a life-giving, life-furthering, and reproducing force, or becomes the killer of life.[2] Reich believed that when an individual is able to surrender to the flow of the energy of life states of heightened awareness and pleasure, culminating in human orgasm, follow. When this flow is blocked, the energy held in stasis in the body becomes a source of neurosis or physical diseases, such as arthritis and cancer. With Reich a clear relationship between mind, emotions, and body was revealed.

The progressive combination of Freud, Jung, and Reich made it possible for Western psychology to begin to incorporate Eastern philosophies and psychologies. These Eastern doctrines, particularly Tantric teachings—which evolved in India and spread to Tibet, China, Thailand and Indonesia—and Taoism, which is an ancient philosophy from China, imply that the liberation of the spirit must be based on the liberation of the entire being. This spiritual liberation only takes place through the full expression and understanding of the nature of human sexuality.[3] As with Reich, these philosophies consider sensual ecstasy as a universal nourishing force. The Jungian concept of archetypal Male and Female had an expanded position in Tantric cosmology: the entire Universe was seen as being built up, pervaded, and sustained by two basic forces that are in intimate and intricate sexual union. Unlike some forms of Buddhism and Hinduism, which seek a liberation of the spirit from the physical body, Taoism and Tantra see the physical body and sexuality as tools for human transformation. In these philosophies, the body is the summation and symbol representing the state of our inner spiritual and psychological development.

To bring the wisdom of such ancient philosophies into the body of psychological theory is to broaden and advance its progress. But theoretical knowledge alone does not always lead individuals to self-knowledge. Great numbers of people still find the sexual aspects of their lives empty, dissatisfying, limiting or self-destructive, perverse, painful, or even dangerous. As evidence, we can look at two extremes of sexual disturbances in males that have steadily increased as social problems. One extreme is the sexual obsession that expresses itself in rape. Figures in the United States show an alarming increase from approximately two-hundred-and-fifty-thousand rapes in 1973 to four-hundred-thousand in 1981. The other extreme of sexual disturbance—impotence or complete male sexual dysfunction—also shows an alarming increase. Both of these extremes seem to share the same psychological causes: fear, anxiety, depression, anger, unachievable fantasy, and negative, dirty, and dangerous associations with sexuality.

In this first chapter, I examine the major options for sexual relationships in modern Western society and the problems that plague each of them. As well, I look at the forces impeding the progress of modern psychology and consider new means to overcome these obstacles.

1·

The Heterosexual Options

One important way a man establishes his identity is by the types of relationships he has with women. Society is based upon a structuring of the male/female relationship that provides men with a set of options by which they can relate to women. The structure of male/female relationships can be compared to that of an architectural structure, which is based upon the spacial opposition of vertical/horizontal. Every builder knows a third principle, a diagonal, is required to strengthen, support, and maintain this convergence as a structure. The third element connects with, or participates in, each of the oppositional extremes. Triangulation, or the law of three, is a Universal principle that can be applied to the analysis of relationships, processes, or states of being. For example, the male/female relationship options can be analyzed by considering two extremes and one intermediate form:

1. The first extreme: (horizontal)
Men who have sexual relationships with an unspecified number of women, with no ties and no commitments.

2. The second extreme: (vertical)
Men who commit and bond to one woman, and one woman only.

3. The intermediate: (diagonal)
Men who have a more or less committed bond with one woman and who have sexual relationships on the side.

SEXUALITY AND SELF / 11

Many men have periods in their lives in which one of the above options is dominant, followed by another when a different option is favored. Others exercise one option for the entirety of their sexual lives. Although the two extremes are the most noticeable sexual formats, the intermediate is probably the most ·common, yet has the least social acceptability. The popularity of these three options seems to shift as well, from generation to generation. In recent history there has been a shift from the prevailing popularity of monogamous bonding in the wartime generations (1920-50) to noncommitted, multiple relationships (from the 1960s through to the 1980s). Individual age and social status also affect the choice of options. Multiple relationships may be the most obviously workable format for the young and attractive; on the other hand, it may be a means of rebellion for those who condemn "middle class morality." Blending monogamous and multiple relationships is the more workable option for the wealthy and affluent, or for middle-class folk who find themselves in either a desperate or daring frame of mind. But most of us, the great "middle of the road," find monogamous bonding the most satisfactory. Within this group there are many fortunate couples who discover a great love and partnership and whose monogamous relationship evolves creatively throughout their entire lives.

Recent research into these relationship patterns reveals serious problems associated with all three. Let us examine a sampling of some of the more important studies in each.

Multiple Uncommitted Relationships. Recent surveys confirm that, in the United States, a large percentage of people suffer from stress, anxiety and depression. Research shows that, in the sexually active age group, sexual permissiveness and the new social roles of the sexes are the major source of these stress-related disturbances. According to Durden-Smith & de Simone, fifty-four percent of men and eighty-two percent of women said they were disturbed by situations related to sexual permissiveness and the superficiality of emotional relationships.[4] To compound the problem, many of those who suffer anxiety and depression related to sexual problems become dependent on harmful sedatives, tranquilizers, and mood-changing drugs. These alarming statistics on the use of legal and illegal drugs are well publicized. Substance abuse has become the greatest public concern in the United States, outweighing nuclear war and environmental pollution.[5] Much of this substance abuse is directly associated with sexual problems.

The information concerning dissatisfaction with "single" sexuality may come as a surprise, in light of the media's exploitation of "the new sexuality," which glorifies its permissiveness simply to sell alcohol and tobacco products. Behind the glorified camouflage of advertising messages lies evidence of a great deal of human suffering and alienation surrounding the new sexuality. The personal columns of newspapers and magazines testify to this, filled as they are with single people desperately advertising themselves like commodities, in search of a relationship. New difficulties for children abound in single parent households. Along with the new sexuality have come soaring divorce rates, alienation and loneliness, declining family values, as well as the gravest problem—the Dark Demon—the new plague of sexually transmitted diseases. Surveys that look behind the facade of advertising and the popular press show that most men and women express a desire to have intimacy and sexuality connected to responsibility, and that both men and women value kindness, understanding, sensitivity, and integrity over sexual excitement when evaluating a relationship.[6]

Monogamous Bonding. What do statistics reveal about men who bond with one and only one woman? For those who look to "traditional sexuality" and "normal marriage" as a way out of the dilemma of modern permissive society, the statistical prospects are not bright. A general norm is that almost one in three marriages ends in divorce and in many urban areas of the United States, one out of two marriages terminates in divorce. Study after study reveals the discontent and frustration of people caught in marital or long-term relationships. One typical study, done by Dr. Helen Singer, points to a phenomenon called I.S.D. (inhibited sexual desire). According to Dr. Singer, people seeking marital consultation or therapy are reporting a reduction in, or complete loss of, sexual desire.[7]

Many psychologists have attempted to pinpoint why normal marriages are rarely as successful and rewarding as one might assume they would be. For the most part, the explanations are similar: couples, unaware, tend to fall into male/female role assignments that have long been programmed by society. In a "typical marriage," these roles have been shaped in a particular distorted manner by various social and psychological factors:

• Conscious or unconscious imitation by the young married couple of the example set by their parents and society in general.

- Romantic illusions perpetuated about love and marriage through music, entertainment, and the popular press, including commercial exploitation of sex, romance, and marriage.
- Repressed or inadequate education on sexual and marital life.
- Puritanical religious views on sexuality.

The result is a male/female role assignment in marriage for which the subscript very often reads as follows:

Women have been conditioned to repress their sexual appetites and to use that energy to pursue protection and emotional and financial security for themselves and their children. Men, in response, have been trained to accentuate competitiveness in pursuit of the tightly withheld sexual prize. The "typical male" has become the perennial performer, driven to proving his manliness, his control, and his power. This male is always eager to succeed, at first in sports, then business—to prove himself worthy to be chosen as a sexual partner by a desirable woman. This victory, though, does not really procure his sexual fantasy because the woman has a different set of priorities, which includes marriage. The male usually adapts to her hidden agenda: the role of protector and provider of a family.[8] A further complexity emerges because the typical modern woman has inherited, from centuries of abuse, a cultural amnesia as to the true nature and power of female sexuality.

This repression of femininity, combined with the male pattern of pressure to compete on a nonsexual level for sexual favors, tends to generate imbalance in the psychological state of the "typical male." Under the pressures of constant competition, a man tends to lose his capacity to express his feelings and needs. He is not allowed to be afraid and is ill prepared to accept failure. His obsessions with success, assertiveness, and performance leave him unable to be receptive, passive, playful, and sensual—in other words, human.[9] Following the open relationships and sexual experimentation of the 1960s, the Yuppie generation has, it seems, resurrected the problems of conventional marriage, stemming from the traditional male role.

Edward C. Whitmont in Return of the Goddess points out that the patterns resulting from these typical male/female roles (that of the aggressive male seeking sexual satisfaction and the dependent, possessive female needing protection) leave men and women with what are called symbiotic relationships. In this form of relationship neither sex perceives or knows each other as independent individuals, but only as projections of their inner needs.

The lover who is motivated only by his need to conquer and to satisfy erotic appetites fails to see and to accord individuality and human dignity to the object of his desires. In turn, the over-mothering or over-protective female likewise acts primarily for the satisfaction of her own needs, regardless of her partner. She is experienced by the man as suffocating and devouring. His instinctual, most often unconscious, response is to love her and leave her, to take flight after he gets what he wants and to discount her as a person. Indeed, she tends to act out of an unconscious possessiveness and the need to express her urge to give and to contain, regardless of whether what she gives is wanted or can be assimilated by the other. (Whitmont, *Return of the Goddess*, p.132)

Dr. Stephen Chang, a Taoist teacher and doctor of Chinese medicine acupuncture, sees the same pressures of stress and performance that Whitmont discusses psychologically reflected in the male orgasm. Dr. Chang describes what he calls the ordinary male ejaculation syndrome:

The male orgasm is analogous to the summit of a mountain. In trying to climb this summit, a man must assert himself physically and emotionally. He must maintain an erection; his prostate must function at one hundred percent capacity; he must pump sweat, endure tension, anxiety and stress and in his need, he must lose a big portion of his nutrients, energy and hormones. Immediately after reaching the summit, the man collapses and falls into a deep abyss of exhaustion and feelings of emptiness, depression, guilt, anger or hunger. Often the results are the man will suffer from dry eyes and mouth, headaches, frequent urination, nervousness, weakness and the loss of a huge portion of his youth (just as if he had emerged from a battle or an exhausting competition). So, according to the old saying, a living lion is reduced in a matter of seconds to a dead dog. (Dr. Stephen Chang, *The Tao of Sexology*, p. 115–16)

Men reenact the role assignment psychologically programmed by society in the physical act of orgasm. Is it possible that different psychological programs could effect a completely different bodily experience of orgasm, and vice versa?

The Intermediate Option. There is no need to document the difficulties of bonding wih one woman and having affairs with others. The crimes of passion and the jealousy, neurosis, and deception that result from the complexities of this type of relationship fill not only the daily newspapers but soap operas, films, and novels. The wife and mistress system, which seems to be an effective solution against the confinement of marriage in certain classes of European society, has never found a successful adaptation in the New World countries due to their Anglicized morality.

In conclusion, our examination of the three options for heterosexual relationships indicate the need for fresh insights and an increased understanding and cultivation of our sexual nature. A signpost to new approaches may lie in the recognition of the physical depletion associated with male ejaculation. The concept, from Eastern philosophies, of storing vital energies has not yet been assimilated into Western psychology. The importance of this factor for the growth and evolution of a sexuality for our everyday lives is discussed in more detail in Part 3.

Meanwhile, the three options held out to heterosexual men (freedom/variety versus love/marriage, plus the intermediate) seem to be marred by serious problems. How are these problems aggravated and perpetuated? Let's examine two major factors that, in modern society, act directly and subliminally upon sexual energy and attitudes: commercialism and advertising on the one hand, and religion and science on the other. Looking at these factors, separately and in combination, will help us to understand how our sexuality has been exploited, blocking the much-needed evolution of male sexuality and becoming a source of major social and political problems. These obstructions and problems can be seen to be created by either an ignorant or a covert and devious use of the concept of archetypes found in Jungian psychology by commercialism, religion, and science.

Sex and Selling

Since the earliest shadows of prehistory, humanity has always created and revered images. Making images and signs is the behavior that most distinguishes us among the rest of living creatures. Modern psychology has shown that, through images, mankind externalizes and becomes aware of its inner nature.

The word "man" or "human" is derived from the Sanskrit word, *manas*, which means "those who reflect upon themselves," and this is perhaps the most important function of imagemaking. The projection outward of our inner content, through powerful concrete representations, acts to clarify values, behaviors, characteristics, and life-roles toward which individuals can grow and develop. In ancient times, these often mysterious idealizations were communicated not only in visual images but through myths. These traditional stories reinforced the collective stereotypes that helped society maintain a connectedness with the spiritual and natural forces that pervade the world.

History warns us that there can be a dark power involved in the image-making process as well. Certainly Hitler and the Third Reich in their rise to power played upon deep archetypal images of the German collective unconscious. The symbol of the swastika, for example, was almost universally held by ancient tribal religions to be most sacred; to them it signified the unrelenting vortex or vulva of the ever-creating/ever-destroying Earth Mother. Most certainly, the Third Reich consciously adapted this symbol to touch a sublimated primitive core in the mass psyche.

Similarly in our modern society that image and mythic process has been taken over by corporations that directly control advertising and, indirectly, the entertainment industry. Powerful erotic images are used for the sole purpose of stimulating consumer demand. The rich, the powerful, the sexy, are images that dominate popular advertising and entertainment, along with other stereotypes such as the "Football Captain," "Good Provider Whose Home Is His Castle," "Devoted Mother," the "Hard-Working Blue Collar Worker," "The Husband Who Can't Even Boil Water," etc. Underneath these modern versions are the same archetypes found in ancient myths: the Armored Knight, the Divine King, the Alluring Harlot, the Virgin Mother, the Devoted Slave, and the Tragic Clown. All these images are employed for the sole purpose of selling consumer products; the side effects of this commercialization have a profound impact on the sexual imagination and identity of vast numbers of people.

The Armored Knight. One example that greatly affects male sexuality and self-identity is the exploitation of the male archetype of the Armored Knight: the warrior who wins self-esteem and feminine favors through defeating and injuring others. The psychological syndrome connected with the commercial exploitation of this male archetype is as follows: throughout their very impressionable adolescence (eleven to perhaps twenty-five years old), men are bombarded by the advertising, media, and entertainment industries with images of a particular type of female beauty—the Model Starlet type. The sexual fantasies of boys are then directed to a very narrow image of female beauty, one that is hyperstimulated and exploited commercially. This female type, for many boys, is in reality virtually unobtainable. Women who fulfill this narrow image of beauty then become like "biological celebrities" in relation to the boys in their adolescent peer groups. At this impressionable age, boys learn that they must compete, like a battling knight, against other men for these desirable women. Generally, the boys' chances of gaining attention from this type of female are dependent on performance achievement and success, in sports and, later, in the world of business. The pressure is further compounded since adolescent girls are usually attracted to older boys who are better equipped to achieve and perform in sports. The commercial fantasy usually implies that the boys should make sexual contact with as many women of this particular genre of beauty as possible. In later life, this male adolescent fantasy is difficult to reconcile with the primary request of many women, which is that men become monogamous as well as become breadwinners for their wives and children.[10] In other words, marriage abruptly changes the mythic image that prevails over a man's youth—that of the Armored Knight—into the mythic image of the King or the Householder. Before we examine the implications of this change, let us examine the effects of the knight image on male psychology.

The important patterns generated in our society by the commercial exploitation of the Armored Knight can be summarized by some of the research and ideas of Warren Farrell in *Why Men Are the Way They Are*. These patterns not only inhibit the evolution of the male self-image, but they perpetuate those male traits that alienate most modern women: men come to rely on competition and aggressive performance as a way of gaining admiration and attention from females. (It has also been argued that a subliminal goal of male competition is admiration from fellow men, but we will assume the primary intent is to attract females.) This paradigm, male competitor with female as reward, generates three main attitudes in men toward women:

1. An underlying contempt, due to the idea that the woman is no more than an object-like prize;

2. Subjugation of that prize to the will and ownership of the deserving victor; or
3. As with all trophies, isolation of the woman on a pedestal.

The domination of the competitive image does more than shape the male/female pattern: it also forces particular relationships of men with other men. We find a disproportionate dependency on male camaraderie resulting from the amity generated from having or projecting a male enemy in common. Recent disturbing riots at soccer and football matches are testimony to this phenomenon. Large groups of males are united against a common enemy (the fans of the opposing team). Usually fortified with a ritual consumption of alcohol, these groups, bonded by a common image, turn the sports arena into a battleground. To ensure that the excessive male camaraderie associated with competitive sport is not misinterpreted, the male groups tend to have strong aversions to, and a paranoia about, homosexuality. Business competition subliminally bears the marks of the same male values, attitudes, and bonding patterns as found in competitive sports. This competitive emphasis not only tends to exclude companionship with women from these activites but contributes to a "war mentality" among most men, including many of the men who make the economic and political decisions that affect every minute of our lives.

Testosterone is the male sex hormone responsible for aggressive behavior. Testosterone levels in the blood rise even from the observation of situations or images of aggression and conquest. These heightened levels engender excitement, hostility, anger, irritability, and aggression and, at the same time, aggressive sexual appetites. The fear and anxiety surrounding the winning and losing of money in business competition have a similar effect on raising adrenaline and testosterone levels. The businessman's expression, "I made a killing today," is less metaphorical and more descriptive than we would like to realize. In tribal societies that emphasize the warrior caste, such as the Masai in Africa, males preparing for battle will frighten and torture a wild male animal, so that the adrenaline and testosterone levels in the animal are raised. The young warriors will then kill the animal and immediately drink the blood, transferring this chemistry of aggression into their own system.[11] Modern athletes repeat a similar pattern when they dose themselves with cortical adrenal hormones and testosterone before competitive games like football and boxing.

For the most part, the people in advertising and commercial

entertainment who manipulate and exploit the aggressive, subjugating, archetypal male images are unaware of the powerful historic and metaphysical forces that stand behind and propel the effectiveness of their activities. In Whitmont's words, "Behind every mass movement or change in the pattern of society, there is an archetype which acts on the imagination of people." It is important to examine how the exaggerated competitive instinct in men affects their relationship to women, the formation of society, and our relationship to the environment in general. The same aggressiveness and need to control and subjugate, promoted by competition, lie very close to the cause of the ecological crisis.

The Divine King. The Divine King represents the energy of expansive creativity, noble sacrifice, production, and accumulation only for the aggrandizement of the spirit of the people. This powerful male archetypal image has been commercialized to generate yet another pattern that fundamentally affects the nuclear family. The nuclear family is a creation of the last three or four hundred years.[12] It replaced the wider extended family, such as the clan, the village, and the caste. In older societies, these groupings gave people a much wider and richer range of interaction. In suburbia, the growing middle class has been sold the illusion of the aristocratic life by the architects of economic expansion. Every suburban home becomes a castle, every man becomes a king over his own domain, very often a tyrant; every woman is a man's queen, very often isolated and bored. The sterility and isolation of suburbia has so stressed the nuclear family that it is falling apart as the basic structure of our society, with no real replacement in view. Religious groups and conservative elements in society seek to salvage this family unit. As the foundation upon which our entire society is built, the nuclear family has well served the needs of systemization and control required by the complexities of industrial societies, but it has contributed little to mental health, security, and general human happiness. The word "privacy" shares a common origin with the word "deprivation," and for ordinary people "privacy" is just that: a cutting off from the joys of collective work, gatherings, and ceremonies. Behind the bewildering sterility of New World suburbia is the reflection of a misappropriation of the mythic force and image of the Divine King.

In the 1960s and 1970s, groups of American males, in response to the Vietnam War, became acutely aware of the devastating hold that the images of the Armored Knight and the

Divine King had on the masculine psyche. Artists, academics, and students inspired what became the goal of many men: to do away with their archetypically male "macho" attitudes and become more receptive, more in touch with their archetypically feminine nature, and to express their inner feelings. The "nurturing male and house-husband" image, which became quite prevalent in American society in the 1960s and 1970s, was much less developed in Europe, and almost nonexistent in Australia. But with the 1980s, the Reagan era, and the emergence of the now infamous Yuppie generation, the return of the aggressive, competitive, male value system pushed the receptive male image into the background and applied to it the label "wimp." It is apparent that the remodeled psychological attitudes and modified sexual roles of the 1960s and 1970s were not sufficient to eradicate the negative influence of these archetypes. We see everywhere the return, with vengeance, of the Armored Knight and the Divine King: the massive corporate takeovers; the outlandish ambitions and conspicuous consumption of the upwardly mobile generations; the news broadcasts that constantly display a fascination with war, business competition, sports competition; and the bizarre media obsession with the Olympic Games. The influence of these two archetypes is formative in our scientific method, our philosophies, and our concepts of God; it lies hidden in the way we use language and mathematics, as well as the ways we consider our body and spirit. Only by revealing the deep structural influence of the Armoured Knight and the Divine King, on all these levels, will men be able to acquire physical and psychological attitudes and disciplines that can weaken the excessive hold these two archetypes have on male sexuality and the male psyche.

Consumerism: From Divine to Demented King

Another obvious parallel between commercialism and sexual attitudes and self-identity can be seen recently in American society. In the 1960s, the American economy changed from being predominantly a production economy to being predominantly a consumption economy. This change corresponds to a mutation of the Divine King image. The original Protestant work ethic, which maintained that the dominance over land and the acquisition of wealth determined one's place in the afterlife, is derived in part from the Divine King image. When this noble, self-sacrificing image degenerates into one that represents the pursuit of personal possessions and an indulgent satiation of desire and greed, we then have the societal image of the Demented King. Just prior to the 1960s, the industrial process began to turn out a vast excess of goods. To keep the economy growing, it became necessary to remove the old ethic of saving money, conserving and maintaining materials and equipment, and the associated frugality of postponing gratification. Advertising, armed with society's new liberalism concerning sexuality, moved into high gear, creating endless needs and desires and in general teaching people to consume. This shift toward materialism occurred at the same time as the emergence of the sexual revolution. Society adopted the goal of instant sexual gratification. At the same time we noticed a relaxation in the laws concerning pornography and the appearance in the media of articles advising sexual freedom and liberation. The new ethic became spend, consume, allow no desire to go unsatisfied, either material or sexual. With the credit card society now established, a rapid consumption of both goods and sex ensued. Little attention was paid to the exhaustion of natural resources or the stress on the social, spiritual, and ecological fabric of life caused by this constantly expanding economy.[13]

At this time the media lured women away from their biological and natural roles as mothers and wives and, under the banner of liberation, pulled great numbers into factories and offices. This commercial manipulation is well described in Bruce Holbrook's *The Stone Monkey* and is traced by him to the 1950s, when numerous sociological studies commissioned by government agencies in Washington suggested methods to restimulate the faltering, consumer-based society. Several of these studies, in particular those by sociologist and social planner Vance Packard, noted that women spent money much more easily and utilized consumer credit systems more readily than did men, who were more likely to save. Social planners suggested that a resurgence of consumerism would result from women having independent money derived from employment. Coincidentally, the beginnings of a feminist viewpoint that stressed the association between "female liberation" and females being employed began to appear.[14] This association may not have been a deliberate manipulation but rather a result of the concurrent relaxation of sexual and consumer inhibitions. However, the result has been, in the last thirty years, an enormous influx of women into the job market and the breakdown of traditional female roles in the family. Consequently, as predicted, the 1960s and 1970s have seen an enormous upsurge in credit spending and an enormous decline in the percentage of savings by families. The manipulation of sexual roles provided the desired stimulation of consumerism.

These economic manipulations have brought about great turmoil and suffering in male/female relationships and great changes in sexual identity. In the three hundred years since the beginning of the industrial revolution, factory, clerical, and retail employment has not represented liberation for males. On the contrary, it turned males into drones and wage slaves. Can we really believe that this vast economic manipulation will ultimately constitute liberation for the female?

The problem may be more clearly stated like this: there is a difference between a medicine and a cure, between a means and a goal, between a journey and a destination. There is no fixed way for masculinity and femininity to interact or relate; it is always a vast universal game of balancing and proportion. All illness, all ignorance, all distortions in the universal balance occur through excesses or deficiencies. This is true of our own bodies. For example, excesses in cholesterol produce one type of illness, while deficiencies in Vitamin C or B6 produce another. In the case of excess the cure is reduction or elimination; in the case of deficiency the cure is supplementation. During this crumbling phase of male-dominant society, women battling for equal status in all areas of life represent a temporary, necessary medicine, but it is not a cure and therefore not the ultimate goal. There is a much greater challenge facing humans. The major battle of that challenge is the balancing of sexuality and its influence on the way each individual exists in the world.

2.

Civilization, Sexuality, and the Sacred

In contrast to the present commercial exploitation of sexuality, the Christian Church, since the period of Gothic Europe, has projected the idea that spirituality is of much higher value than physical material life. In the Christian ideal, renunciation of sexual desire leads to the ultimate achievement; repression of one's erotic nature is itself a key to virtue and higher understanding. Robert Brian suggests in *Friends and Lovers* that the combination of "puritanized" love and frustrated sexuality with marriage is a uniquely Western contribution to the evolution of human relationships.[15]

Modern day commercialism and Christian denial each distort the true nature and value of sexuality in life. They are each powerful enough to prevent large numbers of people from ever really finding the powerful values that are inherent in their sexuality. Present problems in male/female relationships arising from the so-called liberation of sexuality, the Sexual Revolution of the 1960s, are proving to be in many ways as detrimental to psychological and physical health as the legacy of repression from our European Christian sources. This, coupled with the ominous threat posed by AIDS and other sexually transmitted diseases, is suggesting to many a return to the moralistic sexual repressions of our immediate past. But is this return really feasible? Even in the face of existing confusions and dangers, a return to this repression now could be a deadly detour not only for human society but for the human spirit. There is at least one other alternative to a return to sexual repression: to embrace the idea that each human being has access to an ecstatic core of existence and that the primary entrance to this state is through his or her sexuality. This is the acceptance of sexuality as a form of sacred communication. Religions such as Christianity, Judaism, and Islam, which are antierotic and which encourage sexual repression, are forgetting or ignoring the fact that all religions originally sprang from fertility festivals and other rites connected with sexual powers. Circumcision rites are sexual in origin, Easter is a fertility festival, and Holy Communion ceremonies are remnants of rituals that have a sexual union at their base. In fact, the symbolic meaning of a man in front of an altar is that of the phallus in front of the ovum.[16] In ancient esoteric philosophies, sexuality was predominantly a metaphysical and highly spiritual involvement, as well as being a key to understanding the magic and mystery of nature.

Beyond Reproduction

The view that the main purpose of sexuality is simply for reproduction is barely three hundred years old and unique to Western philosophy and science. No ancient civilization that I have researched considered reproduction to be the primary role of sexuality. The reason for degrading sexuality to the level of an animal instinct can be traced to the same philosophies from which arose the puritanical religions, that openly sought to divorce sexuality from spiritual development. Their doctrines, developed to assure the expansion of populations in Christianity and Islam, were then adopted by the orthodoxy of Darwinian biology. This is a topic well covered by Wilhelm Reich in his very emotional essay, "The Murder Of Christ."

Darwin, basing his evolutionary orthodoxy on the already existing Christian view, perpetuated the idea of sexuality as being simply an animal drive for reproduction, no different from the desire for food or sleep. The simplest practical analysis allows us to see that there is a marked difference between sexuality and these primal drives. After all, without food or sleep the organism dies, which is not the case with sexuality. It is also obvious that the sexual drive in humans is completely different from that in animals. It is "natural" for a man to desire and make love at any time. His sexual drive is free from the seasonal bonds of sexual excitation that exist in animal reproduction. Thus, the German philosopher Klages wrote in response to Darwin's theory of sexuality: "It is a willful falsification to call the sexual instinct an instinct for reproduction."[17]

It is interesting that so-called primitive people never attributed the begetting of children simply to the coitus or the union of man and woman moved by sexual desire. The Australian Aborigines have a belief in the Spirit Child—that fertilization occurs from the projection of conscious energy.[18] Among many tribal people, reproduction is considered a possible outcome of sexual activity, but it is not regarded as the basis of sexual desire, nor of the heightened states of ecstasy associated with sexual union. These Australian tribal views are consistent with those of ancient Eastern philosophies, which held that sexual love had a higher form that was independent from, and not reducible to, biological reproduction. In fact, Tantric thought holds that ecstasy destroys the capacity of the sperm to fertilize the female.[19]

This same view is held in some more recent modern philosophies. To quote Julius Evola from *The Metaphysics of Sex*:

> It is unthinkable to associate the exalted models of human love in history and art, such as Tristan and Isolde, Romeo and Juliet, Paola and Francesca, with a happy ending and a baby, or rather a whole brood as a crowning feature! A character of d'Aurevilly says about a pair of lovers who have never had any babies: "They love each other too much. The fire burns, consumes, and does not produce." When asked if she was sad because she had no babies, the woman answered: "I don't want any. Children are only useful to unhappy women." (p.14)

I am not intending to diminish the importance, nor the joys, of having children, but rather to emphasize that this function has been used to obscure the spiritual aspect of sexuality. Procreating is a profound responsibility, and it is equally tragic that in our society fanciful, ignorant, and commercially exploitative notions often distort attitudes about marriage and the conception of children.

From Evola, again, we draw the idea that:

> It is only sexuality through which ordinary mankind in body and mind can rupture illusions and lead to some kind of opening beyond the conditionalities of

everyday life. (Julius Evola, *The Metaphysics of Sex*, p.18)

It is certainly freeing and provocative, especially after all the conditioning of our education, to think that the goal of human sexuality is not only to procreate but also to reach other levels of consciousness and experience. Like meditation, sexuality may release us from the constancy of our thought processes and allow us to feel a transcendental energy within our own bodies.

Male Sexuality and the Female Orgasm

If sexuality can serve both reproductive and higher purposes, we can imagine two different forms of sexuality, each with a different goal: one of procreation, one of self-creation. We can illustrate this by considering the differences between the male and female orgasm.

In general, the present form of Western sexuality is centered on the male orgasm. Surveys show that a large percentage of women do not achieve orgasm: between five and ten percent of women never experience orgasm of any kind and another thirty to forty percent experience it rarely or intermittently. Many women feel that orgasm is not as important as other aspects of sexual intimacy. They feel that the female orgasm is only a potentiality, not a necessity. Often achieving orgasm requires skill and consideration on the part of the male and a sense of trust on the part of the woman.[20] Consider a few interesting biological facts. First, male orgasm is necessary for reproduction, while the female's is not. Further, the most intense pleasure for the male occurs precisely at the moment of ejaculation. In other words, this type of pleasure is the motivating force leading the male to the reproductive event.

Many early Eastern civilizations, and so-called primitive societies, in their social conventions and religious practices, are dedicated to the feminine principle. In societies in which all women are said to experience orgasms, there is either prolonged foreplay in which the clitoris plays a big part, or as in the high cultures of the East such as India and China, there is a consciously prolonged intercourse.

In primitive societies such as that of the Mangaias in Central Polynesia, for example, boys begin their sexual education at the age of thirteen to fourteen under the tutelage of older men. During this period, the boys begin to learn the physiological techniques that prevent ejaculation and that allow them to sustain sexual activity for as long as it is necessary to achieve the female orgasm. Following their training from the older men, adolescent boys continue their sexual tutelage from the older women. They learn the techniques of pleasuring women and acquire a very detailed knowledge of female anatomy, superior to that of most general physicians in the Western world.[21] These techniques of withholding or prohibiting the male ejaculation were of primary importance in the Tantric and Taoist philosophies of ancient Chinese and Indian civilizations. Almost all of the psychophysical disciplines generally referred to as "yoga" emphasize the development of this sort of skill in men.

What is the evolutionary role and significance of the female orgasm, since it is not reproductively essential?

We can distinguish two forms of sexuality. One is centered on the male orgasm, which is predominantly functional for reproduction. The other is centered on the female orgasm, which is associated with the idea that sexuality and ecstatic states are instrumental and necessary for people to obtain an opening to the spiritual world and for their own spiritual development. If this is so, the female orgasm is the door that allows both sexual partners to enter ecstatic states of consciousness through which an identification with the creative power of the universe can be formed.

I can think of nothing else that could more rapidly change the self-image of humankind than to reverse the view maintained by modern science and religion—that sexuality is only an animal/physical procreative drive—and to reinstate the ancient spiritual interpretation of sexuality. Ancient philosophies from India, China, and Greece maintain the view that sexual love embodies an impulse to go beyond the restrictive world of duality and to restore the primal state of Unity. In all these philosophies, sexual ecstasy was considered the basis of magic and the highest spiritual experience. It has the power to transfer extremely subtle psychic drives, powers, and experiences directly into the metabolic and chemical levels of the body, thereby bringing these spiritual energies to the deepest core of our being. Here, perhaps, lies a key—a view of sexuality that can trigger a transformation of identity in both individual and social man.

Resistances to this transformation are deeply ingrained in the mind, brain and body of humanity. Along with the commercial and technological programming, our self-created society forces us into sexual roles and behavior patterns that are in conflict with our biological and evolutionary nature.

Anthropologist Lionel Tiger, as quoted in *Sex and the Brain*, summarizes the source and depth of our resistance to further change:

> Our self awareness about our physical and biological nature has been considerably weakened in modern Western culture. Our own bodies have become industrialized by the Industrial Revolution. We have internalized the Industrial system and the Industrial image in our minds, our psyche and our body. We have developed an arrogant anti-nature, anti-biological attitude through which we are disturbing the physical nature of the earth and undermining our own physical health and well being. In our indiscriminate use of drugs and vices and environmentally injurious technologies, we are failing to recognize that we are a part of nature. (Durden-Smith, *Sex and the Brain*, p.221)

The earth is being bathed in acid rain. Forests, lakes, rivers and the underground water supply are dying of pollution. Huge holes are opening up in the atmosphere allowing in destructive radiation. Toxicity, depletion, and exhaustion cast a pallor over the face of humanity and the Earth. The great Earth-Mother goddess, Gaia, is calling out for a rebalancing of the psychosexual energies.

3.

Toward a New Sexuality

To effect a change in psychosexual energies, we need an education that understands the spiritual as a natural component of our sexuality; with this as a base, we must re-structure our relationship between ourselves, our society, and the natural world. But first, that education must overcome the destructive patterns and repressive sexual attitudes that have been imposed on our psyches over the past three hundred years. The history of Western psychology shows that as the ego develops and grows, so does the physical repression and erotic deprivation of an individual. Ashley Montague's *Touching*, a study on maternal-infant contact, shows us how this begins with an extremely noticeable drop in the amount of body contact and sensual enjoyment that is allowed to occur during the first few years of life. The strong sense of the individual ego prevalent in Western society, the basis for our feeling alienated from nature, is purchased at the expense of sensual enjoyment. Up until the last several centuries, the mother and child relationship was such that they were never physically separate for the first several years of life. They slept together, and feeding was dependent on spontaneous hunger rather than prearranged schedules. Breast feeding continued for at least two years.

Ashley Montague maintains that, in all mammalian species, a healthy adult life is not possible without a large amount of tactile stimulation during the first few years of life. Indeed, the development of the nervous system is dependent on the touching, holding, and carrying that occurs during this period. In fact, myelinization (the formation of a fatty sheath of protective tissue around nerves) does not occur without tactile stimulation.

In a great number of cultures and eras up until contemporary times, the physical stimulation of children was a necessary and an enjoyable activity of adults, which included extended nursing and direct caring. In Bali, for example, the child is carried on the hip or in the sling and is in almost constant contact with the mother for the first two years. Even the gentle manipulation of the infant's genitals by the parents is a common practice.[22] This practice continues in many so-called primitive societies where parents typically play with the infant's genitals while it is bathing.[23] During the Middle Ages in Europe, physical contact with children's private parts in public was an amusing sort of game that became forbidden only when the child reached puberty. These practices are still widespread in many Islamic cultures. This background gives us some indication of how radical the desensualization of children in the West has been during the past two or three centuries of the industrial age. We can even say that industrial and scientific progress seems to have gone hand in hand with dehumanized practices of childrearing.[24]

Montague, as cited in Berman's *Reenchantment of the World*, says further that the existential anxiety characteristic of the schizoid personality can itself result from the lack of tactile stimulation in infancy. Montague writes:

> At the moment of birth the cord is cut or clamped, the child is exhibited to the mother and then is taken away by the nurse to the baby room called the nursery, so called presumably because the one thing that is not done in it is the nursing of the baby. Here it is weighed, measured, its physical or any other traits recorded, a number is put around its wrist and it is left to howl away to its heart's discontent. The child is subsequently put on a fixed feeding schedule that is maintained for months which has little or no relationship to its own hunger pains. Rapid weaning from the breast is encouraged by modern science if indeed the child is breast fed at all. (*Reenchantment of the World*, p. 75-76)

These insensitive and inhumane modern birth practices arise from attitudes that began to develop in the Middle Ages: that body contact between individuals and an individual with its own body are "bad." The behavior patterns that evolved from these negative attitudes toward touching and physical contact in human relations, beginning with the mother/child relationship, spawned the psychological conditions of separation, alienation and disassociation.

These changes are summarized by Morris Berman in *Reenchantment of the World*, drawing from the work of Phillip Aries:

> Prior to the late sixteenth century, neither the nuclear family nor the child existed as concepts. Until the twelfth century, art did not portray the morphology of childhood and portraits of children were almost non-existent until the end of the sixteenth century. The seventeenth century literally 'discovered' childhood and made the point of demarcating it as a stage in a series of separate phases of life. Far from implying greater care for infants, however, this demarcation involved greater alienation from them. Special children's clothing was now used to make visible the stages of growth and, at the end of the sixteenth century, there suddenly emerged a great preoccupation with the supposed dangers of touching and body contact. Children were taught to conceal their bodies from one other. In addition, it was now believed that children should never be left alone. The result was that the adult became a sort of a psychic watchdog, always supervising the child, never fondling it—a practice that is really the prototype of scientific observation and experimentation.
>
> These same patterns were institutionalized in the colleges of the late Middle Ages, where they took the form of constant supervision, a system of informing (i.e. spying) and the extended application of corporal punishment. The birch replaced fines as the predominant penalty and the students were commonly whipped in public until they bled. By the eighteenth century flogging occurred on a daily basis in England where it was viewed as a way of teaching children and adolescents self-control. (p.192-93)

It is interesting to compare these statements with the early observations of anthropologist Sir W. Baldwin Spencer on child-rearing practices of the Australian Aborigines. In the Aboriginal camps, Spencer heard the children "hour after hour, laughing and shouting at their play." He found their freedom emphasized by the lack of any form of physical punishment for transgressing custom or normal social relations. Among all the tribes with which Spencer had intimate contact, he found that there was "certainly no need of a Society for the Prevention of Cruelty to Children." (*Wanderings in Wild Australia*, p.189) He described their education also:

> Out in the scrub with their tiny digging sticks they mimic the action of their mothers, and at an age when the white child is learning to read books, they are busy, unconscious to themselves, learning to read the book of nature. They gradually come to know where to find the bulbs and seeds that are good to eat, and recognize the tracks of every animal, large and small, that burrows in the ground or nests in the trees. (*Wanderings in Wild Australia*, p.190)

In contrast to these tribal examples, the following passage provides comments by Berman and Aries on European childrearing practices and their effects on society and sexuality:

> The late Middle Ages thus saw an abrupt shift in the emphasis of childrearing practices, a shift from mothering to mastery which was one aspect of the emergence of a civilisation marked by categorization and control. As childrearing practices reveal, Western society was still heavily sexualized down to the sixteenth century. It was "the essentially masculine civilization of modern times," as Aries put it, which discouraged nurturing practices. The rise of the nuclear family, with the man at the head, reached full expression in the seventeenth, whereas the crucial unit had previously been "the line" that is the extended family of descendants from a single ancestor. With the evolution of the nuclear unit, the soft heterogeneity of communal life began to disappear. Distinctions were made within the family and between families. The medieval household, which might hold up to thirty members of the extended family, began to shrink and become uniform. Beds, which used to be scattered everywhere, were now confined to a special room. What we would call chaos was in effect the multiplicity of realities, a "medley of colours" says Aries, and it is still observable in streets of (say) Delhi or Benares, where eight types of

transport and forty different types of people can be seen on a single narrow street. (Berman, *Reenchantment of the World*, p. 197-98)

"Masculine" civilization with its desire to have everything neat, clean and uniform, erupted in full force on the eve of the Scientific Revolution. From the thirteenth century onwards, the power of the wife steadily diminished, the law of primogeniture (the eldest son has exclusive right of inheritance) being a prime example of this. Down to the mid-sixteenth century, no man save the occasional astrologer was allowed to be present when a woman gave birth. By 1700, a very great percentage of "midwives" were male. "Professional" civilisation, the world of categorization and control, is a world of male power and dominance. (Berman, *Reenchantment of the World*, p. 225)

These passages reveal precisely how deeply embedded our current system of sexuality is. The patterns of male dominance and sexual inhibition have their beginning even further back in history than either of those two authors suggest. I shall try to reveal how those origins can be traced to the threshold of prehistory. There we may discover the foundation for a reeducation in sexuality that can begin to confront these resistance patterns. This education must first attempt to: (1) offset the pornographic distortions to which young males are subjected from advertising and the media; (2) alleviate the burden of guilt and repression about sexuality from religions and the institutions of this society, and (3) help males get in touch with their real potential to understand and channel their sexual energy, so that it may be a source of pleasure and transcendence for themselves and their sexual partner.

We can look to ancient sources to perhaps rediscover the components of this education. Basically, the shift must be away from any restrictions—religious, moral, or legal—associated with sexuality and it must be toward an emphasis on education in health, hygiene, and the beauty of the physical body. The components for this education are now available within our society. We discover every day the sources of our physical and erotic self-destruction contained within our diet, medicines, and "recreational" drugs such as alcohol, tobacco, and caffeine—the result of our work and lifestyle choices. Modern psychology has

already lifted, for many people, the veil of guilt slung over sexuality by religious dogma. The way is open for a genuine sexual
transformation, far beyond the reactionary revolution of the
1960s.

Self-Identity and Transformation

The transformation of self is an important, but not inevitable,
consequence of self-identity. Self-identity is an extension of the
external identity we arrive at through membership of various
groups. It is the formation of a relationship between inner consciousness and our external life. Jung described this process as
the soul constantly discovering images outside itself that correspond to inner visions or ways of being and becoming. These
images allow our life to take on a particular form or a succession
of forms that then dominate the pattern of our life choices.

Transformation occurs when participation in the unfolding
of one's identity becomes more and more conscious, rather than
unconscious. The whole idea of a creative, conscious participation in the development of our identity mushroomed in modern
Western psychology with the introduction of Eastern philosophy. Almost without exception, Eastern spiritual doctrines
(yoga) provide disciplines and methods for achieving this participation. We can see the result of Eastern influence in the countless human potential and awareness movements. One important
self-discipline that, I believe, could enable many modern men
to participate in the transformation of both their sexual and self-
identities relates to a broad category of practices referred to as
biofeedback. Basically, with the tools of biofeedback, an individual can transfer a bodily function normally controlled by the
autonomic or unconscious nervous system to the conscious control of the central nervous system. One prime example is high
blood pressure: usually blood pressure rises and falls due to autonomic responses and neural signals. The entire process normally
takes place without our conscious awareness. Blood pressure,
among other things, rises as a result of stress and, for some people, to dangerous levels, affecting the functioning of the heart.
Through biofeedback, patients with this problem can be trained
to detect the autonomic reactions leading up to the high blood
pressure syndrome. With further training, the patient can employ a conscious destressing action, such as deep breathing or
calming visualizations, to consciously control the blood pres-

sure response. Many other unconscious bodily functions can be brought under conscious control in a similar way.[25]

This seems like a simple little procedure, but it has vast implications. Jack Schwartz, the well-known clairvoyant and author who for many years worked with biofeedback researcher Dr. Elmer Green from the Menninger Foundation, was able to control autonomic body functions such as blood flow and healing responses. Dr. Green filmed Jack Schwartz, under strict laboratory conditions. In one experiment Schwartz punctured his skin creating a bleeding wound; he then, through concentration alone, stopped the blood flow and, within a matter of minutes, healed the wound without a trace. Gaining conscious control over unconscious body functions was an aspect of many Hindu schools of Yoga. There are numerous scientific records of Indian yogis who could consciously slow down heartbeats and respiratory functions to such a degree that they could remain buried alive for days. All of us, at an early age, were encouraged to exercise control over our autonomic nervous systems when we were toilet trained. Gaining mastery over urination and defecation is the passport to becoming a member of human society. Disciplines of this type can be seen as a powerful tool for self-development, as well as an important factor in shaping society.

Recently, there has been a deluge of guidelines and techniques, appearing in books and magazine articles, concerning the refinement and cultivation of physical activity and the psychological attitudes of men toward their sexuality. Many of these writings listed in the Bibliography, are here presented with a precautionary note from Alain Danielou: "There are two types of dangerous books in the world: one type gives a philosophical overview of the world, but with no means for the individual to implement that view into his life. The other, is a book which teaches methods, disciplines or daily practices without revealing the overriding implications of those practices."[26]

A large amount of this literature is based upon ideas drawn from ancient Eastern texts that have very often been popularized by contemporary teachers through the "counter culture" press. These Eastern methods are founded on the same principles as the biofeedback techniques mentioned above. Many Eastern philosophies emphasize that conscious control over body functions, particularly those that are partially conscious and partially unconscious such as breathing and blood circulation, affords the individual a greater self-mastery, presence, and power in the world.

Techniques such as these may be used to separate male orgasmic response from ejaculation. This practice can transform sexual attitudes and sexual performance. We have already quoted Dr. Steven Chang on the relationship of stress/depletion in male ejaculation to some of the negative psychological patterns in male/female relationships. In the following chapter, we will explore this more fully, as well as how the change in male sexuality associated with this discipline can benefit society and increase spiritual awareness.

II·

SEXUALITY AND THE SPIRITUAL

ROADMAP: DEFINITIONS

The word *spiritual* has been used and abused in recent years to the point that its meaning is either completely personalized or obscured. As with similar words such as *love*, it is often necessary to set forth a specific definition to convey an intended meaning. *I define spirituality as all our efforts to become more conscious of the energies and entities that exist outside of our normal perception, including those normally immeasurable aspects of our own inner nature.*

We live constantly in relationship to unseen or unperceivable energies or things. For example, no one has ever seen a thought, an atom, an emotion, or gravitation. There is no doubt that they affect the perceivable world, and there is no reason to believe that there are not other unperceived factors acting upon us. For example, our bodies are made up of certain quantities of water and fat and substances like lime, calcium, carbon, nitrogen, phosphorus, etc. Within a period of seven to twelve years every molecule of our body is destroyed, eliminated, and replaced, in some cases many times over. There is as yet no explanation as to what the formative force is that enables these molecules to be constantly replaced, while we maintain a consistent form and identity.[1] Some biologists speculate that there may be some invisible organizing field that obliges molecules to maintain position, purpose, and identity during the ever-changing phases of our lives. Even the constancy of our identity may depend on some invisible formative causation.

An important book by Daniel Goleman, *Vital Lies, Simple Truths*, describes how our perception is diminished in order to reduce anxiety. In other words, the nervous system "trades off" awareness of threatening or unfamiliar phenomena to maintain or reduce levels of pain and anxiety in the system. There are whole ranges of experience in our environment that we are either conditioned, or educated, to be unaware of.[2]

When a designer makes a rendering to draw into consciousness an imperceptible intuition or inspiration, it is no different from a tribal person drawing a diagram of a spirit energy associated with water or a wild animal. In this sense, science and spirituality share the same fundamental origin. Since the beginning of history, signs and images of one type or another have been used for the purpose of making visible an otherwise invisible world. Another example is music: a series of musical notations written on a page by Beethoven centuries ago, when translated into sound, for generation after generation, makes an undetectable emotional energy tangible and living. We add to this list drama, ritual, and more particularly, ritual sexuality.

4·

Symmetry and Sexuality

Human sexual behavior, I contend, is based on certain simple laws of symmetry and form, such as the universal law of three. It may seem a very simple idea to try to perceive the nature of things by examining the qualities of its underlying form, but the application has powerful results for our understanding. The laws of form, relating to circles, squares, and triangles, are of a universal nature. They shape the relationships between all entities, both physical and mental. Human relationships naturally assume basic universal patterns: the mutual attraction of lover and beloved is a pattern of "twoness" or polarity with all its intensity and exclusivity. The bond of mother, father and child is a triangle, and so on. Fourfold human relationships are structural and energetic, like a square, and differ from threefold relationships in both the physical world of structure and the analogical world of thought.

Polarity: A Twofold View of Sexuality

According to Carl Jung, our sexuality itself connects us to the unperceivable realm of the universal archetypes of Absolute Male and Absolute Female. The Jungian concept of archetypes, due to the use of complex psychological terminology, is often difficult to understand, but going back in time, we find Plato offers a simple explanation of this same concept: there are hundreds, perhaps thousands, of different types and varieties of chairs in the world, some big, some small, some wooden, some plastic. In addition to all of these specific varieties and types, there is the pure, intangible idea of Chair or Chair-ness. The Chair Idea is a pure functional concept, to which all these different types of chairs owe their existence. The intangible idea of Chair is the archetype. According to Plato, all qualities and forms that exist, both living and non-living, have a pure, absolute state or archetype, from which all the specific types arise. All living and nonliving things, therefore, proceed from an idea, or pattern. The same follows for our understanding of "God" and the spiritual within us.[3]

The premise that an intangible stereotype precedes all the types, varieties, forms, and qualities of things is very often overlooked in popular books dealing with sexuality. The idea of Absolute Male and Absolute Female can project our identity, as well as our sexuality, into a universal domain. Living becomes a constant game of balancing these archetypal sexual energies, first in men's external relationships with women, then with other men. Then, as Jungian psychology suggests, men must also acknowledge, balance, and harmonize the internal feminine quality—the anima. Likewise, women must balance the internal masculine quality, or animus. The same balancing act, occurring in the course of our individual life, occurs on a larger time scale in the evolution of human society.

Absolute masculinity and absolute femininity do not exist without each other. They are a relationship of opposites, just as the idea of dark does not exist without that of light. The imbalances in masculinity that we have discussed, such as excessive rationalism, competition, aggression, and the need to control, exist not only in men, but also in women. The efforts that many women have made to usurp, imitate, or express those masculine traits cannot ultimately be helpful in the crisis of sexuality. These imbalances are found equally in men and women, and the attempt by certain feminist writers to scapegoat men for the entirety of our sociosexual problems is merely a diversion from a possible course of rectification. It is important, therefore, not to ignore the archetypal dimension, because it connects us to the mythic and spiritual dimensions. The underlying premise of most spiritual philosophies is that mankind is not fundamentally dissimilar from the powers and plan upon which the universal creation is based—all share a common lifeforce, called Eros (sexual love) by the Greeks. Through an opening and understanding of our sexuality, this mythic or metaphysical dimension can be seen to exist in each one of us.

Abodes of the Sexual Archetypes

Bodies. Many of the major differences between men and women, on an archetypal and psychological level, are symbolized physiologically by the sex organs. The male sex organ, the penis, is external to the rest of his body, whereas the sexual organs of a woman go deep into her innermost physical center.[4] The male sex organ seems relatively limited and detached from his body and there seems to be a psychological gap between his whole body and his genitals. This apparent detachment from his sexual center corresponds to the abstract tendency of male psychology and mentality. In a certain sense, he seems to objectify or view his own sexuality as separate from himself. This degree of detachment allows men to either abuse or deny their sexuality more easily than woman, hence the sublimation or rechanneling of male sexual energy (as in soldiers, athletes, and holy men) is more successful and complete. Whereas, it is not possible for the absolute female to consider her sexuality as an energy separate from herself. Therefore women's sexuality cannot be easily catered to or organized in external ways. Sexual repression, or rechanneling, in woman very often results in a blockage of development or expression, producing almost a neutral state. In Hindu thought it is said that the female herself is not other than sexuality, she is sexuality itself. The ancient Latin proverb *Tota mulier sexus* means that the whole woman is sexuality. The interdependency between the Universal Feminine and sexuality is notably evident in societies dominated by female energy and organization, such as the tribal, Earth-Mother societies. The Australian Aborigines, the oldest form of tribal culture, developed their entire life so that it reflected the archetypal qualities of the Creative Spirit Ancestors. For all women in this society, sexuality was their birthright: As soon as they reached puberty a full sex life began and it continued until death. They married and had children very young, and if their husband died, they moved on immediately to another. Even at a very advanced age, they were considered (and considered themselves) to be sexually attractive. Often older women became wives and sexual partners of much younger men. All of the women's rituals, songs, stories, and dances were sexually based. In the pre-contact tribes of the western Aboriginal desert there is no evidence of female sexual inhibition, frigidity, sterility or perversion. The nonsexual feminine qualities, such as those found in the old crone, spinister, matron or nun, were nonexistent. On the other hand, Aboriginal men were prevented from marrying until they were relatively older, sometimes forty years of age. Tribal law believed that men must earn their right to marriage and sexuality through self-development and spiritual awareness. The men did not remain celibate during their initiatic years, but marriage or constant sexually attached relationships, were considered, detrimental to their development as men.[5] Every example of an Earth-Mother society reveals a ritual and culture completely preoccupied with sexual symbolism and meaning. Beauty and sensuality are the primary collective pursuits that predominate in time and energy over any technological involvements. The preoccupation with sexuality in the Earth-Mother societies does not mean sexual indulgence. Instead, it means a deep understanding of the power and implications of sexual energy in the organization of life.[6]

It must be remembered that when we contrast these qualitative differences, we are talking about the *Absolute Male* and the *Absolute Female*, not any actual individual man and woman. We also need to remember that each individual man has some elements of the female archetype (anima) within him, and that each individual female contains some mixture of male elements (animus).

While the male may tend to have greater capacities for logic and reason, a woman very often operates through deep intuitive and sensitive qualities of awareness. This is consistent with the symbolism suggested by the difference between men's and women's genitals. The archetypal female does not separate her ethical and logical judgements from instinct, sentiment, and sexuality—that is, she cannot easily separate an abstract mental system from life itself. Archetypal males, on the other hand, have the ability to set up abstract systems of intellect, ethics, and logic. Such differences extend even to the function of memory. The male tendency for recall is governed by an intellectual impulse towards logic, which has its basis in the principle of identity, i.e., *A equals A*. His memory activity contains in it the ideal of logic, which is based on drawing together abstract relationships, making comparisons, and affirming synthetic connections between apparently unlike entities. His perception and memory tend to record and retain information that will support this psychological and intellectual propensity. His memory formations, like his genitals, are often more disconnected from his body. They resist, and are separate from, a stream of inner sensations, perceptions, feelings, moods, and emotions that originate in the flow of experience coming from his body. On the other hand, women have a memory and psychological process that, like their genitals, is completely connected to and absorbed in life. It has a vital nature and is linked to the duration and the flow of bodily experience, inward and outward. It is also connected to the subconscious mind: that "feeling" nature. At certain times it throws up distant recollections, unexpectedly and involuntarily.

These types of fundamental differences are reasons why men and women must be understood in terms of completely different standards and values. In the Western world, there has been a great tendency for women to be measured on value scales that are only applicable to male psychology. This is particularly evident in the modern business world, where women are often considered by men to be devious and unethical in their business transactions. This is because the female memory and intellect will not cling rigidly to abstract proposals and agreements, but will shift position relative to the flow of events. This is very often bewildering to the male mind, which accepts arbitrary, external commitments as *faits accomplis.*

In spite of these differences, many women in modern society are entering the world of career and business under an illusion of social and economic egalitarianism. They are subjecting themselves to a system of values that is applicable to the ideal of Absolute Male and are thereby doing a great violence to their own selves and to their femininity. They are denying and destroying their feminine qualities, which are necessary in their relationship with men. The extreme of this attitude can be seen in the increasing numbers of women now seeking sex change operations. Initially, female-to-male sex changes formed only a tiny portion of the sex-change operations, but by 1988, psychiatrists in this field estimated that about twenty percent of their transsexual clients were biological women wanting to become men.[7]

These important and fundamental variations in the intellect and memory of Absolute Male and Absolute Female also explain the different relationship that men and women have to truth and falsehood. The quality of Absolute Woman is described in the Chinese doctrine describing the primary polarities of creation, Yin and Yang. Yin is the Cosmic Feminine. It is receptive, yielding, weak, soft, mutable. This tendency in women to express in their psychology the cosmic principle of mutability makes their relationship to the truth quite different from that of a man's. Ancient texts state that telling lies is an essential characteristic in female nature. Dr. Otto Weininger, the first

European psychologist to apply metaphyscial principles (the transcendentals of Kant) to the male/female psychology, has observed that nothing is more baffling to a man than a woman's response when caught in a lie. When asked why she is lying, she is unable to understand the question. She may act astonished, burst out crying, or seek to pacify the situation by smiling.[8] The Absolute Woman has little understanding of the ethical and absolutist view of lying. She has no fixed position to accepted fact. The masculine idealistic codes concerning truth and falsehoods, such as those found in Islam stating that lying damages the very essence of one's being and constitutes a crime even worse than killing, is nonsense to a purely feminine psychology. An archetypal feminine mind knows that a lie, a deception, is a great natural weapon. She has needed to employ it down the ages as a protection for her own physical weakness and for the weakness of her brood in their vulnerable infancy.

Theatrics, disguise, and acting are essentially attributes of the psychology of the Absolute Female. Great male actors have a capacity to release this feminine power from within themselves. One could say the higher aspect of the activity of deception is art or the aesthetic pursuits in general. The desire to embellish, to decorate, to adorn, is always more dominant in societies in which feminine energy expresses itself more strongly. Indigenous tribal societies, which usually have an Earth-Mother spirituality, spend large portions of their time and energy on dance, music, and decoration. Women of the Ndebele, a matriarchal African tribe, continue to embellish their bodies and homes with bold, remarkably rich and vital paintings, designs, and beadwork despite great adversity and poverty. These women seem compelled to reiterate their procreative power in the recreation of the trees, flowers, birds, and colors of nature.[9] It's also interesting to note that the word *cosmos* in Greek shares the same root as the word *cosmetic*, as if the universe were only the adornment of the body of the Creator.

Extreme mutability explains why Absolute Woman is prone to "lie" and disguise herself, even when she has no need to do so. It also explains how the propensity in modern women to use cosmetics and elaborate clothing styles is linked to their deepest and most genuine nature. Such behavior is a counterpart to fluidity and mutability in the cosmic feminine nature. This self-protective flexibility, when judged from a male-oriented value standard, appears as a lack of logic and ethics. The quality of mutability in the Absolute Female psychology can also appear as an extreme degree of cruelty. The no-holds-barred cruelty of

SEXUALITY AND THE SPIRITUAL / 47

feminine psychology is again traceable to the protective instinct of the Absolute Female, who is prepared to commit almost any act of deception or destruction in order to protect her young. This type of instinct reduces the kind of commitment she can make to any external ideal or ethic. The feminine may prize in men the qualities that are based on ethical or logical value systems, the heroism or idealism or even asceticism that is often exhibited in male behavior. Women can find the Hero, the Scholar, Saint, or other life roles, motivated by fixed external ideals, very attractive. A woman's recognition and appreciation of these qualities comes not from a direct identification with these elements of the character of the Absolute Feminine, but from an attraction, which is very often sexual, to a specific quality in a particular man. In other words, Universal femininity is sexually attracted to these complementary qualities in masculinity, without the slightest desire to identify with, or emulate, them. When an individual woman does emulate these masculine qualities, it is through her inner masculinity or animus.

Thus women tend to desert commitments to the fixed premises of any system or ideal, to follow truths based on innate drives or subjective feelings. The male pattern of deception or "lying" is the inverse. Men will tend to, consciously or unconsciously, deny anything but the singular perspective that valorizes or defends some fixed system or allegiance. Male religious or political debate is very often like an armored conflict between men "hanging tough" to their precommitted viewpoints. This competitive fencing very often becomes more important than the discovery of the truth. Another form of male "lying" in our society is due to the fact that men are programmed to "cut off" experiencing or expressing their true inner feelings. This habituation to falsify or hide their inner "felt-truth" becomes ingrained in male communication patterns as constant defensive or deceptive tactics. This is particularly evident when men communicate with each other. Tribal society avoided this pressured male deceptiveness by initiating men in elaborate rituals that provided them with genuine emotive release. In our society this fundamental falsification leads to the pervasiveness of corruption in male-dominant social and political institutions. The process of clearly identifying both the essential biological and psychological differences between men and women could lead to much more productive attempts to organize society around the male/female relationship. Although we are presently blinded into thinking that our social institutions are for the purpose of sustaining commercial and industrial activity, the real basis of human society is the male and female relationship. The male orientation, which presently dominates social organization, tends toward abstractions upon which to build that order. Further back in history, male-dominant society acknowledged the fundamental difference between male and female, but judged femininity on some abstract standard to be inferior to the masculine. More recently, male society has replaced that view with another abstract principle, that of egalitarianism, which claims that men and women should be considered the same and equal. As long as we apply male egalitarian concepts to our understanding of the male and female relationship, we will continue to build mechanistic and inhumane societies. Life is enriched and intensified through the amplification of differences. Egalitarianism, when applied to sexuality, tends to neutralize and diminish the very dynamics upon which life is based. What is needed is an acknowledgement of difference, but with no prejudiced attitudes of the superiority or inferiority of either sex.

Brain/Mind. The physical differences in the male and female genitals and the corresponding psychological differences of Absolute Male/Absolute Female are supported on even deeper levels of the body. Scientific research has produced increasing evidence that fundamental differences in the functioning of the brain do exist and are completely related to Male and Female sexuality.

As reported in 1980, neuroanatomists at the University of California demonstrated that the left and right hemispheres of the rat brain are not symmetrical. These asymmetries differ for males and for females. When the ovaries are removed at birth, the female brain develops the more exaggerated left hemisphere growth typical of males. By young adulthood, female rats who have had their ovaries removed at birth show a pattern typical of male brains: greater left/right differences than normally seen in females. But why does the removal of the ovary at birth cause a part of the cerebral cortex to increase in size? These sex differences in the brain may be initiated and maintained by sex hormones from birth. Such hormones also appear essential for the development of those brain regions that control sexual behavior.[10]

This brain function division has been associated with universal masculine and feminine traits by many authors, most notably by innovative psychologist and brain researcher Robert Ornstein. His analogy between the functions of the right and left brain hemisphere and the dynamics of the masculine and feminine is as follows:[11]

Masculine	Feminine
Left Hemisphere	Right Hemisphere
Day	Night
Time/History	Eternity/Timelessness
Intellectual	Sensuous
Explicit	Tacit
Analytic	Gestalt
Linear	Nonlinear
Sequential	Simultaneous
Focal	Diffuse
Logical	Intuitive
Causal	Synchronicity
Argument	Experience
Perfection	Integration

Both men and women have two hemispheres, one that functions primarily in a feminine mode, the other in masculine mode. The sex hormones establish our external sexuality, including the formation of our genitals and our associated male and female traits. At the same time, these hormones emphasize or activate brain functions and psychological characteristics specific to our sexuality. Within the brain/mind of everyone lies dormant the psychological potentials of the opposite sex. Thus we see that the structure of our brain gives a physical base to the Jungian proposition that there is an animus (male) inside every woman and an anima (female) inside every man.

These differences extend throughout the physical body. For example, there is a basic metabolic inequality between men and women: women are more efficient at building up tissue metabolically, just as they create babies within their bodies. They also tend to put on weight more easily and have a harder time shedding it if they want to. Men are more efficient metabolically at breaking down tissue, parallel to their discharge of protein, carbohydrates, and minerals during sex. They also tend to lose weight more easily—much to the dismay of their strenuously dieting mates.[12] In fact, in many ancient Eastern societies, men and women were guided toward eating completely different quantities and combinations of food. The purpose of these dietary practices was to help maintain the fundamental differences between male and female energy. In a male-dominated society, which now pushes an abstract facade of egalitarianism, these important guidelines to the health and well being of the sexes have been lost.

Thus, we have seen the male/female polarity is deeply imprinted on psychological and biological levels and extends to the
physical foundations of matter. We next examine sexuality as
a metaphysical law of nature.

The Triad: A Threefold View of Sexuality

The application of universal ideals, forms, and archetypes can
help us understand the nature of sexuality. Every primary quality exists as a polarity of opposites (beginning and ending) and
every polarity creates a triad (for every beginning and ending
there is a middle). For example, with the polarity of positive and
negative, there is the concept of neutral; or with the polarity of
before and after comes the idea of during. This universal fact can
be visualized by noting that when two points are drawn on a
blank surface, a third point is needed to turn those points into
a shape, i.e. a triangle. Two points on a page (a simple polarity),
can generate a line but never a shape (a two dimensional figure).
While a straight line can graphically represent an extension or
duration between poles, it cannot describe a relational continuum which requires circularity and implies a triangle. For example, with the polarity of black and white, the relational
continuum is a gradation. Starting from the pole of pure white,
black gradually increases and white gradually decreases, until
pure black is approached. The reverse is true in the continuum
from absolute black to pure white. The gradient passes through
a midpoint apex where black and white are intermixed in exactly
equal amounts (neutral grey). In the continuum between day
and night, and from night to day, there are the same reciprocal
triangles formed by the midpoints, apex and nadir. See diagram
Page 51. The implicit or actual triangle in a gradated continuum
between polar opposites we shall call a triad. All the forms of
our three dimensional reality are based upon the eternal law of
threeness; height, width and breadth.

We may extend this triadic principle to help us reconceptu-
alize human sexuality. For example; we can say that pre-sexual
and post-sexual are at opposite ends of our sexual continuum
and these three conditions correlate with the maturation phases
of our life, as well as with three basic types of personality formation.

Every individual has a presexual phase of life, and some human beings remain as what we might call presexual psychologi-

cally. Even though we all are bathed daily in sexual images through popular music and the media, there are still a great many for whom sexuality plays a minor and, in some cases, a nonexistent role. Many presexual types have little or no sexual experience outside the most rudimentary: sexuality as a mode for establishing a domestic relationship and for breeding children. For this type of person, sexuality provides no great release of psychic and vital energies, nor is it an arena in which self-discovery or creativity unfolds, as it is for people who are predominantly of a sexual type. Sexually oriented people find that sexual relationships and experience are the key which unlocks the door to their individuality, their creativity, and their spirituality. The third type, the postsexual person, is a rare occurrence in our times and society. These are people who, throughout their lives, carry a postsexual attitude or temperament; they have *evidently* gone beyond sexuality. They *seemingly* have derived in

DIAGRAM 1. SEXUALITY AND THE PRINCIPLE OF THREENESS

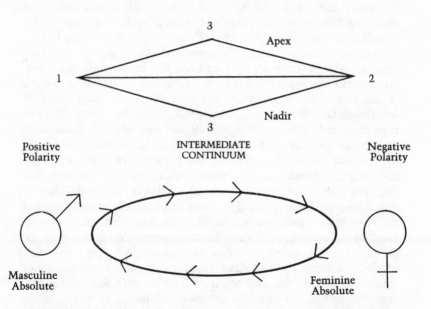

The first analysis of form is into three parts, the Absolute Male/Female polarity and the intermediate range. Since every man and woman is a mixture of Absolute Male and Absolute Female traits, we all fall somewhere on the continuum, depending on the proportion of masculine and feminine qualities that make up our being.

every aspect all that can be gained as a sexually complete and fulfilled human being. The moral attitudes referred to as "Victorian" represent the postsexual ideal. Sexuality is seen as a phase of life which one must endure and evolve beyond in all haste. It should taint one's manner and appearance as little as possible.

There are all sorts of variations and patterns possible in this threefold division of sexuality. Sometimes a presexual stage, a "renewed virginity," can be intentionally reintroduced into one's life as an interim, between sexual phases. This practice very often has a positive effect, providing time to reflect and gather vital forces. However, both sexual and presexual types of people can be deceived into believing they are at a postsexual stage of development. This misunderstanding is aggravated in modern society by the spread of commercial forms of Eastern religions and philosophies. This type of "new age" asceticism and denial is often little more than a subconscious extension of the innate puritanical repressions of European Christianity. There is an enormous difference between spiritual discipline and sexual repression.

When the ancient Greeks said *there are not two sexes, there are three*, they were applying the triadic principle to their understanding of sexuality. This way of thinking suggests that homosexuality, or the appearance of intermediate sexualities existing between the polarity of male and female, is not only a normal but a necessary aspect in the form of sexuality as a whole. Think of the centuries of suffering and confusion that have resulted from societies that have branded the intermediate sexualities as abnormal. It is a perfect example of the way false ideas and dogmas blind people to simple natural facts: every civilization throughout history has evidence of varieties of homosexual or intermediate sexuality. Every individual, in their maturation, goes through a phase of this sort of sexuality. Many past societies, even the most primitive, have acknowledged and utilized the particular talents, sensitivities, and aptitudes that are associated with individuals of these sexual inclinations. I believe homosexuality in recent decades has grown to disproportionate levels in society and to pathological levels in the psychology of some individuals. Because of the crisis in male/female sexuality, many people are turning to homosexual forms even though it is not a deep part of their basic nature. It has been said, There are thousands of people out there who are not gay, they just don't know that they are straight. (See Diagram 1: Sexuality and the Principle of Threeness, p. 51.)

Dual Opposition: A Fourfold View of Sexuality

In the tradition of Plato, the universal laws of form and musical harmony express themselves in all the forms and processes of life. Plato said that everything is dual in its nature, three in principle, and fourfold in manifestation. There are, Plato says, four elements which comprise the manifest nature, that is Earth, Air, Fire and Water. Likewise, there are four basic components in the manifest form of human life, Body, Mind, Spirit, and Emotion. In Diagram 2, I apply this to the range of sexuality, with a harmonic fourfold division of the continuum of sexuality from the Absolute Male, then from the Absolute Female. This duality between male and female and between heterosexual and homosexual creates what I call dual opposition: two sets of opposing sexualities.[13]

Homosexuality also appears quite naturally in the early development of heterosexual individuals. Modern psychology pushes us toward an exaggerated importance of seeing ourselves as separate individuals. During our formative years the source of our identity is adapted from other people, particularly those of our own sex. In other words, we find ourselves by discovering desired aspects of ourselves in other people. This search for self may include either unconscious or conscious homosexual relationships. Unlike ancient civilizations, in which young people could derive their identities from their group (their clan, caste, elders, and the clear archetypes that presided over these groups), modern young people must find themselves through affinities with other individuals. When this gathering phase of youth is completed and the individual identity secured, then it is natural to pass from homosexually oriented relationships to heterosexual ones.

One mythic image that represents choices in sexuality is Leda and the Swan. Both the great Renaissance artists, Leonardo da Vinci and Michelangelo, who were considered to be involved in homosexuality, portrayed this mythic figure. More recently, the symbol was used extensively in Peter Greenaway's film, *A Zed and Two Noughts*. Leda represents adolescence on the threshold of sexuality. She confronts the Swan, who represents the male sex organ, with its long neck and head representing the penis and its soft body the testicles. Bursting forth from eggs, which represent the emergence into sexuality, are two sets of twins, Castor and Pollux, the pair of gods who symbolize and

DIAGRAM 2. SEXUALITY AND THE PRINCIPLE OF FOURNESS

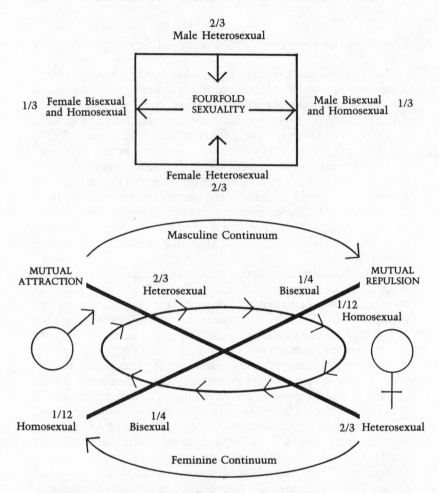

About two-thirds of the continuum toward femininity is composed of heterosexual males, each having an increasing proportion of female characteristics, either on a physical, intellectual, psychic, or emotional level. About one-fourth of the continuum is bisexual males, and the last one-twelfth is male homosexuality. The same is true on the opposite side of the continuum, as Absolute Feminine energy moves toward the Masculine. There will tend to be attractions across the continuum so that, for example, a heterosexual male will be attracted to a female who complements the proportional mixture of maleness and femaleness in his sexuality. As we get closer to the homosexual end of the continuum, the lines of mutual attraction become lines of mutual sexual repulsion, to the point where one would expect male and female homosexuals to repel each other sexually. Bear in mind, though, that these lines of attraction are more complex in everyday life, because each individual has a different mixture of masculine and feminine traits on each of the four levels of his or her being, spiritual, mental, emotional, and physical. Although these proportions, two-thirds heterosexual, one-fourth bisexual, and one-twelfth homosexual, are chosen because they are universal musical proportions, actual quantitative statistics tend to show similar divisions.

protect male homosexuality, and Helen and Clytemnestra, the protectors of female homosexuality. The entire image can be interpreted to mean that the initial emergence into our sexual nature can be marked by seeking our identities outside ourselves in a sexual twin. According to ancient Tantric philosophy, almost all variations of sexual intercourse have some positive and natural role in the fulfillment of human sexuality. It is only an exclusive fixation (or a disproportionate obsession or revulsion) with any one form of sexual experience that can be limiting or destructive in our development.

5·

Sex and History

We have examined sexuality on an individual level from the point of view of polarity, or twoness, then from the point of view of threeness. Now let us return to the dynamics of polarity and observe how it might operate on a broader social and historical level. History, as we shall discover, seems to move through phases in which, for long periods of time, masculine traits are dominant (see Appendix). That is, they are more powerful and are held in higher esteem than female traits, which are secondary and disempowered. During phases such as our own, masculine qualities are encouraged and preferentially educated in both men and women. The most recent research strongly indicates that just before the so-called Historical Age (approximately four thousand to five thousand years ago) the phases were reversed (see Diagram 3 on page 57): Female qualities dominated and male qualities were held to be of secondary value. This alternation between male/female dominance seems to be the dynamic that drives history, just as all progressive time alternates between day and night, warmer and colder seasons. The male-dominated phases of human history are called *patriarchies*, while the female-dominated phases of human history are called *matriarchies*. The metaphysical powers (the archetypes) of sexuality are like two copulating gods: for a while the male dominates and is on top, then they roll over, the female dominates and an era of history changes.

The movement of history can always be reflected in some geometric model. For example, Darwin's theory of evolution pictures history as a straight line moving from past to an unknown future. Almost without exception, tribal societies represent history as a circle, where the ending or conclusion of time closes back on its beginning. In Diagram 3, we utilize the double helix image, with each strand representing the rise and fall of matriarchy or feminine energies, against the oppositional rise and fall of patriarchal or male dominance. Matriarchal energies rise as patriarchal energies fall and vice versa. As one reaches its ascendency, the other is in decline. Within the larger wave cycles, there are small cycles occurring approximately every 50 years, 500 years and 2,500 years, within the 5,000 year cycle. We are now, I believe, at a major junction of these two forces, which accounts for the great contemporary crises in human sexuality, society, and the natural world.

DIAGRAM 3. INTERLOCKING WAVE FRONT (DOUBLE HELIX)

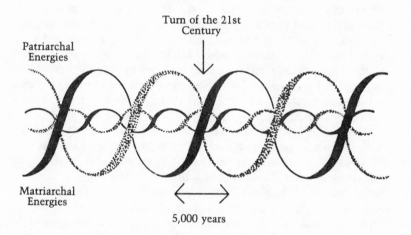

Turn of the 21st Century

Patriarchal Energies

Matriarchal Energies

5,000 years

Let us look at the historical origins underlying the male-dominant sexual, psychological, and social value structures of today. In so doing we begin to glimpse the importance of sexuality to the social and environmental crises that now confront us. In other words, we will position sexuality as the fundamental relationship by which we can view the origins of all human powers and limitations, we will not use it as Freud has done, to describe the subconscious only, but rather see it as the key to the mystery of creation itself.

The Ancient Matriarchy

Just previous to what we call the historical period—the Upper
Paleolithic era extending through the Neolithic—we find human societies holding supreme the worship of the Earth Goddess
or the all-powerful Great Mother deity. The entire physical earth
was held to be her physical body: the hills and valleys were
considered to be her voluptuous breasts, hips and thighs, while
the rivers were the sacred waters flowing from her womb, etc.[14]
This Mother Earth deity was later referred to in Egyptian mythology as Mut, and in Greek mythology as Gaia. Biologist James
Lovelock gave his recent scientific hypothesis the name Gaia
because it considers the earth and its biosphere a single self-
regulating, self-organizing system.[15] This era in history assigned
the highest spiritual position to the Feminine Principle, which
expressed itself in art and psychology as an intimate connection
between humanity and nature. For example, figurations are very
often half bird or animal and half human. There were close
relationships drawn between the qualities of the physical environment of the earth and the qualities of human consciousness.
These were portrayed symbolically through the depiction of gods
and goddesses in later mythology.

Plants and animals were expressions of the living organism,
Earth. Each animal personified both the psychological and living
qualities of the earth, as well as the psychological qualities of
humanity: the ferociousness of a lion, the cunning of a fox, the
slothfulness of a koala. Likewise, flowers were representations
of the most subtle and tender psychic qualities of the mind of
Gaia. The nuances of hopes and fears that we experience as
humans are eloquently metaphored by a rose, a violet, or a lily. In
this way, man's relationship to God and Nature was an unbroken
Trinity, each a symbolic representation of the other. The three
together remained a single, irreducible unity: all of life emerged
from the womb of the Earth Mother, into which all beings returned at the end of life.

The archaeological excavations of civilizations of this period, known as the pre-bronze age cultures, indicate that they
were peaceful, ritualistic cultures. Digs reveal neither caches
of weapons, fortifications, nor large number of skeletons killed
at the same time by wounds. In general, it appears as though
these Neolithic eras were times of deep earth-honoring, integration, and harmony between man, nature, and a sensed and

experienced metaphysical world.[16] While lacking the perfection-ist drives of technological civilizations, they indicate great artistic and spiritual advancements, living in peace and for long continuous periods of time. The Australian Aborigines represent perhaps the most accessible remains of this type of Earth-Mother-dominant phase of evolution. For an estimated sixty thousand years, they maintained a hunting and gathering form of life.

Patriarchy: Rise and Fall

The phase of human evolution dominated by the Feminine Prin-ciple came to a disruptive end a little over five thousand years ago. In three distinct waves, Aryan or Indo-European invading tribes first moved into and conquered the ancient civilizations in the Nile River Valley, then what was to later be Europe and the Mediterranean Basin, including the Greek Isles and northern Italy. These invaders came from the Eurasian steppes and their victories have been cited by the historian Mircea Eliade as being the single most important event in human history. They were nomadic* horsemen who carried with them a culture, a lan-guage, and a world view radically different from that of the older, Neolithic civilizations.

The regions surrounding Persia, from whence the Aryans originally came, we can suppose once maintained large devel-oped societies that declined probably as a result of severe cli-matic changes. There are indications that the region had been at one time warm and fertile and had since grown cold and harsh. Because of the harshness of this environment the Aryans saw themselves in conflict with, and struggling to overcome, nature. They developed a way of life based on nomadism: goods had to be transported from place to place. Because each of these natu-rally integrated regions, referred to as *nomes*, could no longer provide sustenance for its population, transportation and trading of materials became primary. The trials, dangers, and austerities

---

*Nomadism here refers strictly to peoples who traveled between settled areas, trading and transporting goods. It does not refer to peoples such as the Australian Aborigines who, although wandering over large terri-tories, still maintained a deep knowledge and contact with the topogra-phy of their region and an active communication with the spirit nature in rocks, trees, streams, etc.

of the road emphasized the need for masculine traits. The connection with the locality was severed. This was in complete contrast with the earlier, Earth Mother civilizations in which the human population was completely integrated with the streams, trees, rocks, plants, and animals of a particular locality in intimate contact with the spirit nature in all aspects of the physical environment. The psychology of the nomad reduced his sense of God to a transcendent force that either guided or punished him in the labor of his travels. This nomadic psychology, then, is the impulse and origin of monotheism (belief in one God). The singular image of a transcendent god that could be carried from place to place, unrelated to the body and Mother Earth, shaped the Aryan mind.[17]

The needs of the nomadic life also led to the subjugation, or what we call the domestication, of animals by the Aryan tribes for the purpose of procuring a constant yet movable food source. The older civilizations were hunter-gatherers who, in addition to game, consumed vegetal food. Some derived the food from scattered plantations while others harvested the seasonal yield of the natural environment, the earth itself as a garden. The nomads, on the other hand, consumed primarily the dairy and meat products of subjugated animals and foods that could be dried and carried in bulk. Oddly enough, modern agriculture was spurred by the demands of nomadic existence. The degenerating matriarchal settlements began to utilize their knowledge of plants and in particular to cultivate grains, which they traded for meat with nomadic herdsmen and traders. Thus the farmers, in turn, shared the dependency of the nomads on possession and on taming the earth to their needs. One man could own cows, horses, and women, as well as other men. The sense of conflict with the environment and the harsh realities of long migrations were a rule of life, accentuating masculine qualities and producing a patriarchal social system with a chieftain at the head of the hierarchy.

The rise of patriarchy and the destruction of matriarchy has often been cited as the historical subplot of the biblical myth of Cain and Abel—Abel, the nomadic herdsman, and Cain, the sedentary farmer. In my view, the polarity of Cain and Abel encompasses both patriarchal images. They are both descendents of Adam, who himself represents the preceding hunting and gathering or matriarchal phase.

The nomadic-based cultures experienced environmental pressures that affected the syntax and grammar of their language forms. For example, time and space were equated in the Aryan languages with distance and separation, time being rigidly divided into the linear mode of past, present, and future. This is in contrast to the Earth-Mother languages such as Australian Aboriginal or Hopi Indian of the western United States. In these Earth-Mother languages, time and space are continuously interwoven cycles of time that fold in upon themselves and space, with a transparency that resonates between the world perceived internally and externally. In the matriarchal mind there is a metaphorical connection between planets and stars and the rocks and trees of the earth, as well as between the psyches of men and gods.

The relationship between humans and habitation changed within the nomadic minds of the Aryans. Architecture, which in ancient societies seemed to grow organically out of the earth locality became, under Aryan influence, tent-like, temporary structures superimposed upon a submissive and temporarily possessed plot of earth. These same attitudes toward architecture are still evident in modern cities where buildings are imposed on the landscape: tent-like, irreverent to the surroundings. The most powerful contemporary architecture is that of highways, again monuments to the Aryan nomadic impulse. Our cities are not settlements in the ancient sense of the word but merely centers for the exchange, storage and transportation of goods, in other words preoccupations of the nomadic mind. Modern skyscrapers could aptly be called vertical highways.

The Aryans, out of the necessity to travel, became indifferent to ritual and art. They lost the protection and restraint of territorial instincts and they incurred conflict and strife among constantly shifting groups or tribes. This introduced a religious reverence for the warrior. Their highest honor was for a man to die a warrior's death in battle, touched by the thunderbolt of the abstract god of the sky. This patriarchal attitude is still prevalent in the psyche of modern Western males and finds expression in his fascination for sports of aggression and for institutions of government and commerce based on competition and conflict.[18]

The relationship between the Ayran nomadic consciousness and military and totalitarian governments is touched upon by Bruce Chatwin in *The Songlines*:

Any nomadic tribe is a military machine in embryo whose impulse, if it is not fighting, is to raid or threaten. . . . It can be argued that the State, as such, resulted from some kind of "chemical" fusion between the herdsman and planter, once it was

realised that the techniques of animal coercion could
be applied to an inert peasant mass.

Apart from their role as "Lords of the Fertilizing
Waters," the first Dictators called themselves "Shep-
herds of the People." Indeed, all over the world, the
words "slave" and "domesticated animal" are the
same. The masses are to be corralled, milked, penned
in (to save them from the human "wolves" outside)
and, if need be, lined up for slaughter.

The city is thus a sheepfold superimposed over a Garden. (*The Songlines*, p. 202)

Lands are invaded, controlled by force, and the indigenous Earth-
honoring populations subjugated or destroyed. The spiritual or
psychic bonds between humans and the earth is broken: the
earth is exploited, plundered and desecrated, along with feminine energy in general. This process of colonization has occurred
in successive waves, gaining in momentum five thousand years
ago and continuing to this day. Within the period 2,500 B.C. and
1,500 B.C., Aryan invaders first toppled the ancient Dravidian
cities of the Indus Valley and the ancient matriarchies in Sumer,
Babylonia, and Troy. The cycle of patriarchal destruction of
more ancient civilizations reached its epitome two hundred
years ago with the English destruction of the most ancient Earth-
Mother culture, the Australian Aborigines.

Colonization continues today in the form of multinational
commercialization and industrialization, which always sacrifice
regional and local development and culture to profit on a global
scale. Besides colonialism and earth destruction, patriarchy is
always associated with the worship of sky gods. From elevated
transcendental states of meditation to the Christian Heaven in
the sky, the reach is always an upward denial of the earth. Mis-
siles, airplanes, skyscrapers are all male phallic forms, straining
with a limited material source of power to escape the earth.

By using the symbolism of the association of the feminine
to the earth and the masculine to the sky, we can continue to
draw the outlines of this great historic drama from which we
have all descended. Thus we can recognize Zeus, the ancient
Greek thunderbolt god of the sky and Indra, the Indian fire god
of the sky, as the Aryan patriarchal gods who replaced the Earth-
Mother goddesses of the preceding age. The Aryan male experience is one of discontinuity, contrast and opposition, whereas
the matriarchal goddess experience of the world is concerned
with continuity. The older way is nature bound, following the

vegetal dimension of growth and decay in an endless flow that exists only in the here and now. It is a reflection of the will of nature and a submission to instinctual forces. The patriarchal consciousness that the conquering Aryans introduced was, on the other hand, concerned with achieving and idealizing. They encouraged heroic, self-willed expression bent on battling and opposition. Their abstraction of god into a transcendental sky principle strengthened the tendency to abstract in general. God, now conceived as a remote ruler, invisible and incomprehensible, was the prototype for the creation of other abstract hierarchical forms, such as the nation state. This consciousness is also fundamental to the basis of modern science as a method of thinking—completely objective, analytical, abstract and, in practice, life-denying and often ruthless. In his book, *The Geometry of Meaning*, Arthur Young gives an interesting demonstration that contrasts what we can generalize as the ancient matriarchal consciousness with our own predominantly patriarchal form. It goes like this: in an abstract system it is perfectly logical and consistent to make the statement: 1 divided by 2 = ½ and this can be proven by subsequently adding ½ and ½ together = 1. But if you tell a child that he can divide a whole thing in half and put them together again to make a whole, the child may try this out by cutting in half his pet turtle, and he will find that it is true that he gets two halves by the division. But when he goes to put them back together again he will find that he cannot revive or recreate his pet turtle.[19] This illustrates the result of an abstract statement, which is perfectly logical, consistent, and true as an abstraction but which, when applied to life and a natural system, is a disaster.

Historically, civilization and human life under a predominantly patriarchal psychology and life view have been marred by the process of attempting to superimpose abstract systems of government, science, morality, and relationships on individuals and human societies. In many instances, while the Aryans adapted the fundamental structures of a matriarchal world, they retained much of their nomadic patriarchal mindset, causing great contradictions which we inherit today. For example, the matriarchal world, in the later phase, was primarily agricultural, with its social order dominated by women. The Aryans adopted the sedentary agrarian way of life but maintained their male dominance and control from their nomadic past. This hybridization has led to a lot of confusion, inconsistency, and conflict in understanding the male and female roles and the delicate balance in male and female sexuality. This inconsistency is not without benefit, as the unconscious retention of matriarchal formations helped maintain balance throughout the patriarchal historical phase. One such example is the humanizing image of an abstract God the Father giving birth to a human son. These types of ambiguities will no doubt aid in the coming matriarchal resurgence.

One aspect of life that changed radically under the onslaught of Aryan consciousness was female sexuality. The psychology of the Earth Mother did not try to perfect, idealize and abstract, but accepted nature and life as the inseparable connection of opposites. The maternal instinct of nature accepts and decrees the relationship between life and death. It is the Earth Mother, Gaia, the highest principle in the prehistoric religions, that celebrates destruction for the sake of rebirth. In a matriarchal religious view, in order for life to proceed and renew itself, it must also be destroyed.

> Light and dark, joy and pain, cruelty and beauty, are mutually interdependent: nothing can come into existence unless something equivalent goes out of existence. We are motivated, not only by an urge to live, but by an irresistible urge for undoing and destroying. The great maternal psyche is a non-personal power of creativity which perceives that sacrifice is at the very core of creation. Every conscious effort calls forth a corresponding unconscious force. Every so-called good evokes a compensating evil. (Whitmont, *Return of the Goddess* p. 56)

The experience of the union of opposites was reached through ecstatic ritual practices, which were basic to the matriarchal religions. These practices became intolerable in societies dominated by rational, perfecting, abstract structures imposed by the evolving patriarchal rulership and led eventually in Europe to the ugly conflict of the sexes known as the witchhunts.

When the universal male principle of control, rationality, constructiveness, industry, and progress emerged, it could not tolerate the turbulent, subconscious, and chaotic feeling depths of the feminine-dominated mythomagical phase of civilization that preceded it. Here, then, is perhaps the underlying metaphysical cause behind the atrocities and subjugations, that men have perpetrated against women in the past and which they maintain to this very day. The atrocities and subjugations are against not only women, but against the cosmic principle of femininity.

The patriarchal dreams of permanent peace (afforded by massive weapon arsenals), of classless societies, of modern democratic or socialistic welfare paradises, of functional world legislative organizations, of economic systems of productivity and wealth are now revealing themselves as nightmares of alienation, repression, violence, and a degeneration of the human spirit. We are learning that society cannot be founded on abstract, rigid ideas imposed directly on a living reality. The most valued result of this patriarchal world phase is the emergence of an autonomous, self-reflective, self-motivated individual and this may be a seed of light in the darkness. This seed of realized individualization could generate a new evolutionary process that would no longer require the vast, oscillating struggle of the cosmic forces of femininity against the cosmic forces of masculinity. Realized individuals have now glimpsed how these cosmic principles (anima and animus) operate within our own psyche and our own sexuality. Through the magical identification of our sexuality with the primary forces of the universe, we may at last be able to harmonize our sexual patterns, behavior, and energy, both individually and socially. Human sexuality can then reflect a new power, beauty, and understanding, which can beneficially affect nature and the world around us.

In great oscillations of time spanning millennia, the pendulum swings back and forth between a matriarchal-oriented cycle of human evolution towards the opposite male patriarchy, just as day follows night. Or, just as the positive/negative polarity of the earth's magnetic field alternates between the North and South Pole every fifty thousand years. This swing, we have speculated, occurred historically with the Aryan invasions about five thousand years ago. From the Persian steppes, the nomadic patriarchy swept south and west, conquering the declining Earth Mother civilizations in India, Greece, and the Italian peninsula. Perhaps these feminine-dominant civilizations were then in a stage of corruption and excess, just as we today are immersed in the excesses and corruption of patriarchy. Again, it is important to remember that we are exaggerating the negative aspects of patriarchy because it is now in a degenerating phase. At the same time, we are tending to idealize the matriarchy, which now appears as the perfect antidote to the present crisis. In actuality, each aspect of the sexual polarity has its strengths and its limitations. Plato, and other ancient philosophers and historians, noted with disgust the corruption, superstition, black magic, and degradation that they observed during their time in the remnants of declining matriarchal societies. These polar swings between male dominance and female dominance are often marked by disruption and chaos in human life and society, when much is lost and destroyed. It is not simply men who are the conspirators behind the subjugation and repression of women. Men and women alike are instruments of vast swings in an alternating current of psychic energy polarized as masculinity-femininity. This polarity pervades and maintains all of life through continuing cycles in the evolution of consciousness.

6•

Sexuality in Philosophy, Religion, and Myth

Several philosophical traditions develop the metaphysical aspects of human sexuality and help us contemplate the history of our world through understanding the universal nature of our sexuality. Among them is the philosophy of sexuality and love outlined by Plato in his play *The Symposium*.

Plato's *Symposium* is written in a dramatic form. The scene is a banquet attended by an intimate gathering of important philosophers of the time, including Socrates. The old boys, it seems, have recently done a lot of partying and have decided not to get completely drunk, but instead to dedicate the gathering to the meaning of Love. Each guest in turn speaks his mind on the eternal mystery. Many startling viewpoints arise. The most interesting opinion comes when one of Plato's characters posits the idea that masculinity and femininity were originally constructed in one being. These complete individual beings were pictured as being round with four arms and four legs.(The circle, or roundness, and the number four have, in these traditional philosophies, always represented completeness.) At some point the demiurge or creator realized that humanity in this form could become too powerful, so these complete, round beings were cut in half to form two arms and two legs: one was made Male, the other Female. Hence the attraction between the sexes is really our longing to find and regain our completeness.

Although this is rather an unusual philosophical metaphor, it does harken back to pre-Christian philosophies which were based on obtaining integration and relatedness (matriarchy), not individual separation and perfection (patriarchy). One way to interpret the movement of history through these alternating phases is that, during one phase, a particular component of either our bodies or minds is accentuated and developed, to the exclusion of other parts. For instance, during this current patriarchal phase there has been a separating and perfecting of a particular quality. Over the past five thousand years, we have seen an enormous dependence on the utilization of the cerebral cortex, the development of rational thought processes and related physical dexterity. This has been accompanied psychologically by an increase in individual identity and self-assertive will and motivation. In the alternating matriarchal cycles, there should be tendencies to integrate these specialized developments back into the fullness of our own being and into the being of our Earth Mother.

This psychology has been developed by Carl Jung, who demonstrates how sexuality plays an important metaphysical and spiritual role in the completion of the process of individualization. The goal of this process is to become whole, not perfect. The whole person is never blameless, guiltless, or pure, as in the perfecting processes of Puritanical, male-dominated religions. Rather, the whole person is one in whom all sides (the dark, light, big, small, etc.) have been combined. This paradoxical unification of self, which is a combining or harmonization of opposites, is a mystery that can never be rationalized, understood, or comprehended and that leads to a polycentric (many centered), rather than a monocentric (single centered) view of human psychology. A person is never strictly this or that or any one thing but is always a multiplicity of possibilities, that may express contradictory qualities of personality.

The Rise of Monotheism

Modern patriarchal psychology imposes upon us the view that we must organize our personality around one consistent inner core. This moralistic psychology emerged parallel with the concept of monotheism in our spiritual philosophies, which demanded that there be one absolute and singular image of God. Polytheistic psychology and spirituality, on the other hand, allow for the acceptance and appreciation of a whole array of qualities, identities, and energies that pervade, in an endless play, both the inner world of self and the outer world of Nature. In Greek mythology, for example, Demeter was both the symbol of the maternal, nurturing aspects in human psychology, as well as of the rich, black, fertile soil of the earth, along with the rain and sunlight that allows the earth to grow abundant crops. Athena was a goddess who, in human psychology, presented the attraction toward order, organization, normality, and constructive thought processes. In the physical domain, Athena, as the daughter of the patriarchal god, Zeus, represented female energy completely at the service of male goals. She represented urban settlements, homes, towns, and cities. Artemis was the famous female Amazon warrior woman who, according to the ancient Greek historian, Herodotus, shunned cities, domesticity, and contact with men, preferring to live in the wilderness, remote and free from the male-dominated world. In human psychology, Artemis represents the qualities of independence, solidarity, individual self-sufficiency, all that is remote, insular, and virginal.[20] In the natural environment, she represents the wilderness, the aspects of nature that are untamed and wild, like the uninhabited and untouched forests and mountains, areas that are apart and alone. Some of the other gods in polytheism are raucous, vile, lunatic, and unpredictable, but they, like qualities that are expressed in the personality, are accepted and expressed as part of creation. Hence the moralistic dilemma of Good and Evil that arises in the monocentric, monotheistic religions is avoided.

The dominant modern religious philosophies have placed unification with the absolute, paternal God as the goal of spirituality. This includes the Eastern forms of monotheism such as Buddhism. The older polytheistic or matriarchal forms do not suppose the individual uniting with an abstract and absolute God or Being but, rather the search or journey that the ego undergoes in order to arrive at a unity of self. In mythology this is often pictured as a great pilgrimage and adventure that can be painful and full of tests and risks. Part of the achievement of this mysterious wholeness within the self always includes sexual experience and sexual understanding. It is, as in Plato's myth, through sexual love that the wholeness is accomplished.

We can surmise that a radically monotheistic religion, such as that of Islam, in which there is extreme negativity and aggression toward polytheistic religious practices, is in reality a continuation of the destruction of the matriarchal world by the invading patriarchy. In addition, we consistently find, in patriarchal, monotheistic religions, elaborate inhibitions concerning female orgasm, displayed to the extreme in Islam with practices such as female circumcision.

We find in Christianity equally severe and destructive attitudes toward female sexuality, particularly those originally associated with polytheistic initiation rites. In every recorded civilization previous to Christian Europe, it was accepted that women had sexual intercourse with spirits, gods, and beings from other dimensions of consciousness. These civilizations include Egypt, India, China, Ancient Greece, Rome, and pre-Christian Europe. Much of the so-called witchhunts and inquisitions that persisted in Europe from the Middle Ages until very recent times, in which thousands of women perished, were an attempt by the Church Fathers to stamp out this commerce between women and the spiritual world. Having myself viewed a female fertility ritual in a remote village in India, I can begin to comprehend the efficacy of these rituals. Women in entranced, ecstatic, abandoned states evoked, in relation to the earth, a vital, energized expression of the procreative force and power of femininity, so vibrant that one might believe it could affect the fertility of nature. Female sexuality has never been strictly limited to women's relationship with men; it is a powerful force that connects humanity to the fertility and life force of the earth and the universe. The diminishing, the neutralizing, the repressing of these metaphysical aspects of female sexuality by masculine monotheistic Western religions have not only brought great suffering to the real nature and meaning of being a woman, but have inevitably crippled and distorted male sexuality—to say nothing of the almost incomprehensible desecretion brought upon the planet Earth.

Male Myths: Oedipus, Parsifal, and Other Visions

As we mentioned earlier, myths are stories that contain symbolic characters and describe the archetypal Male and Female energies as they act within us and our world. The myths of Orpheus (Christ), Pan (Lucifer), and Dionysus will be later considered in this context. Jungian psychology suggests that there are two myths that symbolize the nature of male sexuality, one from a patriarchal period of human consciousness and one from a female-dominated era. The first is the myth of Oedipus, which is fundamental to a Freudian patriarchal mode of psychology; the second is the myth of Parsifal, which is closer to the Jungian mode.

The Myth of Oedipus. Almost the entire literature for understanding male psychology today is based on the Freudian adaptation of the myth of Oedipus. Granted, this myth has powerful implications for understanding the conflicting dynamics of the influence of the Mother and Father figures on the formation of male sexual identity. We will now concentrate on exploring this myth and its importance, but it would be an impoverishment to hold the variety and meaning of male sexuality to this one archetypal model.

Let us examine first the interpretation of the Oedipus myth as it exists in conventional psychoanalysis. As a young man, Oedipus accidentally kills his father and unknowingly marries his mother, thus fulfilling the oracle at the time of his birth that caused his parents to leave him on a mountainside. His mother kills herself when she discovers what she has unwittingly done. For Oedipus' crimes against both parents, the gods punish him. Freudian psychoanalysts interpret this as follows. The construction of male sexual identity begins with the male infant's enormous biological dependency upon the mother. His mother is the source of life, nourishment, protection, and affection. Naturally, every male infant begins his identity actively seeking to keep his mother and his mother's attention and love all for himself. To become a heterosexual male, this little boy must transfer his love from his mother to another adult woman (bride). This fundamental identity pattern is different for the evolution of a heterosexual woman. The little girl ideally must transfer her love and dependency from her mother to her father and then to the figure of the bridegroom or other adult male. Therefore the path to heterosexual identity is not the same for both the sexes, but both begin by actively seeking to maintain the dependency upon the mother. And both must give up the mother, under fear of castration, as imaged by the myth. Castration is of course intended here symbolically, not literally, and was adapted by Freud as a symbol to describe the paralyzing fear a child faces in surrendering his or her dependency on the mother. It is undoubtedly a problematic metaphor, but one that describes the situation that arises if a young male continues to maintain his mother as the object of his desire and dependency once he has passed through puberty. If this does result, he then comes into competition with his father and feels the threat of castration. Ideally, though, the young male must surrender one object, the mother, and focus his desires and attentions on another object, the bride. In this way he avoids a conflicting situation with his father and instead gains an identity that prepares him to become a father. Oedipus, in the myth, fails to make this transfer from his mother to another woman, and he thus becomes the model for a whole range of problems and perversions in male sexuality. This myth informs us that the pathway to male heterosexual adulthood is one fraught with dangers. For example, if a young male is too submissive toward his father and never challenges him for his mother's love, then he never attains the strength necessary to mount a challenge in order to assume a sexual role with another woman. On the other hand, if the young male attacks the father too vigorously, either overtly or covertly, and refuses to accept the restraint or obstruction that the father is meant to impose upon him in respect to his mother (the castration symbol), then his tendency will be to remain rebellious, infantile and unable to give up his attachment to his mother. These two possibilities correspond with the two sides of a boy's sexuality, or rather his bisexuality. His masculine side seeks the mother and opposes the father. His feminine side may try to avoid the father's threat by taking the mother's place and becoming an object of the father's love or admiration (the obedient son).

In his book, *What a Man's Gotta Do?*, Anthony Easthope has an interesting analysis of the popular religious image of Christ as the model of the obedient son. He notes how disconcertingly feminine the popular portrayals of the face of Christ are, to the point that every feature and quality other than his bearded face is completely feminized. Christ is seen as the Son who remains entirely subservient and submissive to the Father and who, accordingly, becomes a male image with disproportionately developed femininity. Easthope continues:

> Jesus does not marry and his interest in women in the New Testament is not sexual. In many ways he seems more interested in and closer to men, his disciples. Instead of challenging the Father for the Bride, he passively endures the Father's aggressions and is penetrated by thorns and nails (phallic symbols). According to Luke 22:44, Jesus says "Not My Will but Thine be Done". Jesus' passivity follows from the absence of the woman or Mother in a role of creator. The Christian God the Father has no wife, and therefore Jesus has no object of desire to contest for with the Father. In the popular understanding of Christianity, this is the most powerful myth in the whole of the Western tradition. It perhaps

unconsciously celebrates a de-sexualized masculinity
and a son's feminine love for his Father and complete
obedience to him. (p.25)

The enormous philosophical and psychological error that this
myth represents is basic to many of the problems that lie at the
heart of the formation of our sexual identities in the Western
Christian world. To understand this deviation, let us examine
another myth which is now being used by Jungian analysts as
a much more comprehensive model for understanding the inner
development of male sexuality.

The Myth Of Parsifal. Let us approach the notion of mythology
with the idea given to us by Jung and others: that myths represent to us in story fashion patterns of life that are universally
valid, that is to say, *archetypal patterns.* The myth of Parsifal
and the Holy Grail describes the great number of inner problems
and challenges a male must face to achieve his sense of individualization and his complete conscious personality.

The story of Parsifal, also known as the myth of the Holy
Grail or the Grail Legend, is the story of a young man who faces
a succession of dangerous and challenging adventures. It symbolically outlines the great psychological and spiritual problems
he had in finding and expressing his real self, as well as the
complexities and difficulties he had in understanding and fulfilling his sexuality. The myth indicates that the young knight
must face first the shadow or dark side of his own nature. This
unwanted and dangerous side of ourselves conflicts with our
conscious attitudes and ideals of how we would like to see
ourselves. We must reconcile all that is opposite to the desired
appearance of ourselves. The adventures of Parsifal require that a
man confront and include in his self-expression the unconscious
feminine component. The interpretation of this myth opens up
when we apply Jung's concept of anima and animus, that each
human being is really androgynous—that is, we are a slightly
different proportional combination of both male and female elements. Ideally, a man generally identifies with his masculine
side and wears his femininity on the inside, so to speak, and a
woman conversely. The revealing of the feminine elements
within a man is a matter of great psychological subtlety and
difficulty. The myth of Parsifal symbolically reflects these difficulties and intimates that, unless a man can accomplish this
integration, he cannot hope to reach an understanding of his self

or his sexuality. The Holy Grail is the lost chalice of the Last Supper. In the story it is kept hidden within a castle. The knights of King Arthur's court pledged to quest for the Grail after it appeared to them at the round table in a shaft of pure light. Each sets out on a solitary search and each fails due to a defect in his masculine character. Parsifal, the knight whose name means "perfect innocence," sets out and finds the castle as if by accident. The "Fisher" King of this castle suffers continuously from a wound that will not heal. The wound is a reference to the pain caused by the incompleteness of his being. The "Fisher" King signifies the king of the ocean depths, therefore, the relationship of the subconscious mind to the male principle. Parsifal's search symbolizes a search into the depths of the male psyche. Parsifal has the innate power to heal the wound, and set the kingdom in order, by merely asking the correct question; however, he is unaware of this power and is expelled from the castle. He then wanders for five years, (one year for the development of each of his five senses). During his exile he undergoes numerous adventures, and after a long time he achieves his second opportunity to enter the castle and to ask the liberating question of the "Fisher" King. The question that Parsifal asks and that cures the King is "What purpose does this Grail serve?" The question symbolizes the beginning of introspection. The theme of the myth, the integration of the conscious and subconscious elements of the male pysche, makes Parsifal an ideal male model for the coming matriarchal age.

The first conflict that Parsifal faces after leaving his mother is the battle with the Red Knight. The message that his mother gives him on his departure is enigmatic and contradictory. She warns him first never to seduce or be seduced by a fair maiden. This aspect of the message that the Mother projects onto her son involves the repression or diminishing of her own sexuality in order to reduce the attraction between Mother and Son. It is a message that can either destroy or help bring to fulfillment her son's future sexuality. Its negative aspect contributes to the all too familiar attitude that certain men have toward women, known as the virgin/mother syndrome. This makes a man inwardly puritanical about female sexuality, as he views sexually liberated women to be loose or even prostitutes. This type of man will usually marry a woman upon whom he confers the virginal purity of his view of his mother, creating a marital sex life that is repressed and that, very often, soon after the birth of the children, becomes non-existent. The positive aspect of Parsifal's mother's message results when the male applies it to his anima. This message means that a male should not become seduced by nor should he seduce (that is, over utilize or excessively draw upon) the emotional, intuitive, moody, subjective qualities within his own psyche. According to Jungian psychology, the productive relationship a man must develop with his anima is like that outlined in the romance of the Middle Ages: he must be completely devoted to this feminine part inside himself. He must utilize it as an image of his own higher nature, his soul, so to speak. The feminine within is like an incredibly pure and beautiful image to which he can dedicate acts of heroism, virtue, wisdom, and spirituality. It represents a yearning for completion within himself. The urge for the perfection of love through a union with the complete object of one's desire and love is an archetypal drive that transcends physical relationships.

One of the great distortions in Western Christian societies resulted when these attitudes of idealizing feminine beauty and virtue were transferred onto external relationships between men and women. Men repressed their physical and sexual desires for a woman instead of realizing that this applied only as a symbol for relating to their internal femininity. The wisdom and ideas handed down from ancient times in the form of myth and legends were intended only for the conduct of the *inner* life and *inner* development of men and women. When these rules and modes of thought were projected into the external world, the result was a travesty, and very often a destructive disfiguration of human nature.[21] We have seen the gory side effects that resulted from the sexual puritanism that began in the Middle Ages in Europe. When there is an extreme idealization of feminine beauty and virtue, along with associated sexual repression, there arises the exaggeration of female darkness, power, and cruelty. The witch-hunts began within the psyche of the male. This distortion over a four hundred year period, coming to an end in the eighteenth century, saw over four million women in Europe tortured and put to death for witchcraft, an atrocity that frightened and repressed female sexuality to an unbelievable degree, causing imbalances in male/female relationships that we are still attempting to untangle today.

In general, when wisdom and rules of conduct originally intended for the inner development of the psyche are projected onto the external world and external behavior, the results are disastrous. Another example we have already discussed relates to the idea that "all people are created equal." The ideal of a fraternity between human beings was meant originally as a goal of inward realization, of a state of consciousness through which one could experience the unity of mankind. When this concept is taken and externalized as a basis for social dogma and the organization of society, it creates the bureaucratic uniformity and the tyranny of mediocrity that have become the hallmark of patriarchal democratic, socialistic, and communistic societies.

The second half of Parsifal's advice from his mother was not to ask any questions. This attempt by a mother to repress her son's curiosity and sense of exploration is the symbol for that understandable, yet often negative, aspect of the parent/child relationship. The parent often unconsciously attempts to enclose the child in sets of values that are really only applicable to childhood; in other words, to keep the child's development subject to that of the parent. This is further symbolized in the myth by his mother dressing Parsifal in a homespun outfit. This is why if a man is to achieve the sense of himself as an individual and to fully experience the power and transformative magic of his sexuality, he must break his bondage to the mother and to the values that she imposed upon him as a boy. He must break his devotion and sense of obligation to his mother and finally see himself completely separate from her. The paralysis of individual growth that occurs if a man does not make this break is symbolized in Parsifal by his not asking the appropriate question when he first gains entrance to the Grail Castle (his whole or complete self).

All the adventures of Parsifal, after he succeeds in breaking the maternal fixation, have a special significance to phases of sexual development in men. For example, Parsifal has a series of battles with competing knights who each wear a different colored armor. The first of the battles is with the Red Knight (the only adversary he must actually kill) and symbolizes the conquering of the youthful stage of his own masculinity. In the Red Knight phase of development, the male must compete with adversaries on the field of battle, or in the sports or business arena. It is in this stage of life that a man must stiffen the fiber of his character—become strong, assertive, and worthy of a reproductive relationship with a woman, whose beauty and virtue should equal his strength and valor. The myth also suggests that he must outgrow this driving competitive and success-oriented phase of development (slay the Red Knight) in order to reach the full development of his masculinity. It is interesting to note that Parsifal wears the armor of his Red Knight phase over the homespun outfit given to him by his mother. This may be interpreted to symbolize that this phase of development is subconsciously motivated by a lack of fulfillment and conclusion in his relationship with his Mother.

In his book *He*, to which I owe much of the above explanation of Parsifal, Robert Johnson points out that so many men in the patriarchal male-dominated Western society never outgrow the Red Knight stage: the sports arena or competitive business remain the center of their entire sense of identity and self-worth. Both Johnson and Whitmont suggest that Parsifal is the myth that symbolizes how male sexuality must evolve in the coming matriarchal age. Parsifal is almost the opposite of Oedipus, whose life, like that of Christ, is dominated by the Father figure whom he must either obey, replace, or by him be destroyed. This obviously patriarchal myth, used by Freud as an explanation for male sexuality and its problems, is diametrically contrasted to the Parsifal myth: Parsifal is fatherless and, after he has broken the constrictive feminine influence represented by his mother, his life is expanded and guided by women in his search for the Holy Grail. The Holy Grail is the symbol of the fulfillment of his complete self, as well as the symbol of the vessel, the universal receptive feminine: the all-containing Mother of Life. Parsifal has great respect for the mystery of the feminine. He is not in any way the conquering hero, nor the righteous, powerful warrior who must control himself and others through unbending vows and laws of obedience. Instead, Parsifal is the wandering errant knight, open, searching, vulnerable. He is the seeker of love, to whom the finding of love is paramount. In his quest he accepts joy, sorrow, and failure in himself and others. He almost naively explores new ways of relating. He is the spirit pioneer, the researcher of life.

Whitmont says of the Parsifal model of masculinity:

He realizes that the best one can do in any situation is seek, ask, risk and remain open. He accepts a state of flux and becoming rather than hoping to be right, justified and invulnerable. (Whitmont, *Return of the Goddess*, p.194)

Simply said, the story of Parsifal provides a male model that encourages a man to develop by improving himself, rather than by proving himself. The constant wars of self-assertion that mankind wages (the war against nature, the war on viruses, the war on drugs, the war on illiteracy, and the battle against time) all reflect an exclusive devotion to the archetype of male combat, which now has grown to the extent that it threatens us with self-annihilation.

Parsifal's quest for the Grail becomes an attempt to gain an answer from his internal feminine as to what women want in their relationships with men. The mysterious answer that he receives to the question: "What purpose is this Grail meant to serve?" is, "Sovereignty over men!" The meaning of this answer has been interpreted in several ways. I believe it has to do with the cultivation and control that men must gain over their own sexual responses in order to provide themselves and women with the deep, ecstatic joy necessary for the furthering of life. This ecstatic state, I might add, is as necessary for the perpetuation of life as is the reproductive aspect of sexuality. Almost all of the texts concerned with the spiritual aspect of sexual practice describe the activity of the man withholding his ejaculation and retaining and absorbing the waves of pleasure from prolonged coitus. Through this retention, he absorbs from the female the intensity and depth of feeling associated with her orgasm. (This is discussed in detail in Part 3). The transmission of the quality of the female orgasm to the male is basic to the discovery of the feminine power and energy within himself: his anima, in Jungian terminology. This, then, is the physiological basis that begins the process of awareness and the harmonization of opposites within each individual male. His sexuality is a key to the discovery of his complete self, as it opens the door to extremely subtle psychological states that are transmitted and assimilated by the entire being.

Myth and Vision-Transforming

It is interesting to note how mythic stereotypes affect even our scientific evaluation of reality. We have discussed the exaggerated importance given to the male image of the combating warrior. This image has even influenced scientific interpretation of the activity of the sperm during fertilization. The conventional image of a sperm cell is that of a fiercely competitive loner who fights his way upstream against stupendous odds, racing with millions of kin to be the first in planting a dollop of DNA in an egg. Very recently, two scientists at the University of Manchester in England have revised the whole scenario of sperm during fertilization, formulating a much more Parsifal-like image of the sperm's activity. Some sperms seem to play an almost altruistic role, giving up their own chances of reproductive success to help the top seeded sperm in ejaculation. These scientists found that in the rat, after a healthy sperm enters the female reproductive tract, masses of deformed sperm in the same batch of semen bunch together, forming a kind of plug, and die. This plug bars competing sperm from any additional would-be fathers, thereby assuring the genetic victory to one of the first arrivals.[22]

The image of the aggressive, active sperm, which is only now being overturned, has its roots in much earlier attitudes. In the Hebrew culture of biblical times, for example, the patriarchal Sky Father energy gained its subjugation over the universal feminine through the indiscriminate release and distribution of sperm. By means of uncontrolled emissions, men began to widely impregnate women outside the guidelines set down by tribal law. This breach in the understanding of sexuality left women primarily bound to the procreative maternal role and at the same time reduced the power of sexuality to a biological function. The sperm of the Sun King or Sky Father was said to reign omnipotent, assuring the propagation of his descendants.[23]

By presenting semen as the dominant means of procreation, Church and society obscured a tradition of knowledge that existed in all ancient Earth-Mother religions. This knowledge was that, under certain circumstances, pregnancy could be triggered by means other than a male sperm. The Australian Aborigines, for instance, held that procreation occurred in two distinct ways, one called Sperm Children, the other called Spirit Children. The latter were born of an impregnation in which a spirit energy, often related to deceased ancestors, accumulated in features of the earth, such as rocks, trees, waterholes, etc., and took on an active form. This spirit formation could then enter a woman through a variety of portals of the body.[24] This idea of spiritual impregnation, universally held in Earth-Mother religions, was also one of the important secrets of the Egyptian temple. There this principle was symbolized by the parthenogenic capacities of the scarab, whose eggs are hatched from within a dung ball (symbolizing the Earth), without fertilization. The Egyptians believed that this power and capacity, which they observed in nature, represented both the metaphysical mystery of the Universe created from a unitary source, and a latent spiritual capacity in humanity itself. This mystical view of parthenogenesis became one of the carefully guarded aspects of the Dionysian fertility cults. From these sources, the idea was absorbed into Roman Christianity as the idea of the Virgin Birth. Like Christ, men such as Julius Caeser, Pythagoras, and Socrates claim to have been the result of a spiritual, rather than a seminal, conception.[25] The subsequent obliteration by the patriarchy of male initiatory practices of semen retention and female orgastic earth rituals was the means by which the important psychospiritual concept of Spirit Child was removed from human imagination.

With the change in our understanding of the process of conception came the change in our understanding of the concept of death: the idea that our spirit energy after death resides and regathers within earthly and natural forms was replaced by the concept of a spiritual ascent to Heaven. Again, these conceptual shifts diminish our respect for, and understanding of, our relationship to the earth. The shift in our understanding of procreation is aptly recorded in ancient symbols. In several Earth-Mother religions, the symbol for procreation is that of a serpent dripping fluid from its tail into a cup-like vessel.[26] The serpent represents the vital life force of the earth and the cup the female uterus. As the patriarchy emerged and strengthened, the symbol for procreation appeared in Egyptian hieroglyphs as a penis spurting semen, replacing the concept of the spiritual fecundating power of the Earth itself.

Some contemporary American philosophers of sexuality, most notably Robert Bly, are advocating that men who have completed the process of coming to terms with their feminine, receptive nature must now reexamine and strengthen their identity with the father.[27] I agree that men must find a masculine archetypal replacement for the Armored Knight (macho syndrome), but a reinforcement of the paternal figure, I feel, is ill-advised during this transition toward matriarchy. In some ancient matriarchies not only was the concept of paternal conception minimized, but maternal male relatives of the children held the major responsibility and male influence on the children, not the father. This social pattern allowed the child to identify with the line of ancestors through the bloodlines of the mother and, at the same time, reduce the possibility of patriarchal hierarchy in family and social structure.

There are other mythic male images, like Parsifal, which can act as a guide to the roles men may use in relating to women, during this transition in human sexuality, roles that will be more effective in the future than the Armored Knight or the Divine King. The controversial film, 9 ½ Weeks provides an interesting male model derived from the myth of Cupid (Eros) and Psyche. Psyche, the youthful feminine soul, needs to be sexually awakened in order to experience a deepened, more mature sense of her womanhood. Cupid, the image of the anonymous male lover, leads the young woman through sexual experiences that expand her self-knowledge and human compassion. In the myth, Cupid and Psyche have their passionate liaisons only in the dark.

Psyche never sees her lover's face and never knows his identity. It is a passion with great depth, but without the intimacy of personalized contact. Cupid warns Psyche that she must never try to find out who he is, that the power of their love depends upon his identity remaining obscure. One night, after making love, Cupid falls asleep and Psyche breaks her vow by holding a candle to Cupid's face. A drop of wax falls from the candle. Cupid awakens and realizes Psyche has discovered who he really is: the adolescent god of pure sexual love. He then flees. In Adrian Lyne's 9½ Weeks, Mickey Rourke, in his relationship with Kim Basinger, plays much the same role as Cupid. He is adolescent in manner, not a man who can be restricted to a permanent relationship. He maintains a quality of mystery and aloofness that charges and intensifies their shared sexuality. Rourke leads Basinger through sexual interludes that awaken her sensuality, her anger, her jealousy: experiences that humiliate, bewilder, and degrade her, and also ones that elevate and celebrate her beauty, attractiveness, and sexuality. This charged relationship brings about a profound transformation in the woman's personality. Basinger changes from a slick, art gallery career girl, to a woman who finds deep poetic empathy with this pure, aging artist whom her gallery has exploited. As soon as Basinger seeks to find out her lover's identity, that is, tries to reduce him to an individual man with a hometown background, etc., she destroys the mystery and intensity of their romance and the relationship ends. Criticized by feminists and other more conventional camps for its display of raw sexual power, this film can also be recognized as a modern retelling of the myth of Cupid and Psyche. Through it the important role of the transitory, mysterious lover who consciously participates in the awakening and maturing of the feminine soul is brought to life.

Another male myth, the myth of Orpheus, is a combination of the myths of Cupid and Parsifal. Orpheus is a beautiful musician, who uses his great charm and spiritual beauty to try to rescue his beloved wife, Eurydice, from the underworld. This myth, again, represents the role of the male lover participating in the evolution of the feminine. The myth of Orpheus has also been paralleled to the story of Christ, in that he acts as a redeemer for others who are trapped in the world of death and darkness.

The interpretation of the Parsifal myth by Johnson and Whitmont, as well as my interpretation of the Cupid and Psyche and the Orpheus myths, are only some among many possible interpretations. One strength of mythic vision is that it allows us to see many subtle and varied aspects of human sexuality that are generated from the same archetypal stories and patterns. Now that we have compared the patriarchal myth of Oedipus with the matriarchal myths of Parsifal and Cupid, it is interesting to ponder the origins of the story of Christ, which over time took on some parts of the Oedipus myth.

Evolution of the Christ Story

One of the fundamental themes of the story of Christ is that his physical body is resurrected into a state of immortality. This event is presented to the rest of humanity as the goal of our evolution. The theme of the resurrection or rebirth of the body can be traced much further back into ancient Egypt to the myth of Horus and Osiris, who suffer death but are perpetually reborn. The mythic ideal that death can, and will, be transcended to obtain immortality has been a source of inspiration for millennia. It is a view held by many ancient tribal peoples, as well as one of the underlying motivations of modern science. The Australian Aborigines, for example, believed that death is unnatural and always due to an accident provoked by magic. Medical science, in a subliminal way, holds a similar view, by assuming a resistant and denying stance in the face of sickness and death.

Many of the other major elements in the story of Christ are derived from the older myth of Dionysus, the great erotic god of female sexuality worshipped throughout the world during the preceding matriarchal age. The myth of Dionysus was the first to contain the idea of a being that was crucified, descended into the world of darkness, and was reborn. This myth was also the first to contain the idea of a human woman (Semele) as a mother who was not impregnated by a human male but by the inspiration of God the Father, Zeus (the Immaculate Conception). In one version of the Dionysus myth, the mother was also drawn bodily into Heaven (the Assumption). Dionysus was born among the animals just as Christ was born in a manger. The ass which Christ rode upon when he entered Jerusalem to achieve his destiny and the palms that were waved by the people are also symbols that were, thousands of years before, sacred to Dionysus. In ancient Dionysian ceremonies, the image of Dionysus was always placed on an ass and palms were waved by the celebrants. The ass was sacred to Dionysus because of that animal's legendary sexual voraciousness. In St. John's Book of the Apocrypha, Christ is depicted leading his twelve disciples in a symbolic ecstatic round dance, a Dionysian ritual. These are but a few of the similarities of the two myths, indicating how the minds and forces which helped establish patriarchal society and religion throughout the world were drawn to use and distort the structures and images derived from the myths and rituals of the earlier matriarchal age.

As discussed earlier, myths are models for explaining the inner working of our own psyche. They are pictures of the forces and energies involved in the emotions, feelings, and thoughts that dominate our lives. Historically, when the Savior of Humanity, Dionysus/Christ, is changed from one who excites the deep ecstatic states of feminine sexuality into Oedipus/Christ, the celibate obedient son of an all-powerful, abstract father figure, we can expect that human beings will develop a far different sense of what constitutes their salvation, their happiness, and their own inner nature. Those who, in any era, control the means of communicating and propagating models and images also control the shape and destiny of the society. From the time of Egypt through to the Middle Ages, massive communal architecture and ritual (the Mass) were the primary means for communicating the dominant psychological images of a people.

Today, dominant psychological images are conveyed through films and non-ritualized theater. We can be justifiably alarmed when the Savior figure being perpetuated in the imagination of the population is Christ/Rambo, an image symbolizing aggression and repression.

7.

Repression of the Feminine

Feminine sexuality, as it existed before the centuries of repression, is almost opposite to what modern women are programmed to experience in terms of their sexuality. It is recorded, even in European history prior to the Medieval witchhunts, that women express a boundless, lusty sexuality, one that far exceeds that of men. Many ancient philosophies state that women have a far more powerful and intense sexuality than men. It is for this very reason that female sexuality has become more repressed: the female sex organ is internal, penetrating and reverberates deep within her physical body. A man's sex organ, like his sexuality, is more external to him. Any repression of male sexuality cannot deny or ignore the physical presence of a constantly recurring erection, nor all the sensations and inevitable responses to that erect penis. On the other hand, the non-visible female genitalia can be more easily ignored and the feelings associated with it blamed on subjective inner feelings—feelings susceptible to imposed self-incrimination and guilt. Under the external repressive forces of religion and society that have acted upon human sexuality, it seems that in women the greater the depth and intensity of innate sexuality, the greater its repression.

As an interesting anecdote to this theory, it was revealed in a recent sexual research survey that men between the ages of twelve and forty think about sex on average six times per hour; between twelve and nineteen years old it is twenty times per hour, that is, once every five minutes; and even between the ages of thirty and thirty-nine it is four times per hour. These statistics were originally used to verify the feminist position that men are subconsciously obsessed with sexuality. That was the case until a similar survey, done with women, revealed higher averages of sexual fantasy in every age category.[28]

The repression of the Absolute Feminine has ramifications for the Absolute Male sexuality. *Remember, sexuality is a continuous energy flow. Suppressing one quality of that sexuality at any one point in the continuum causes the reappearance of that quality in an exaggerated form at another point. The repression of femininity in women in the Universal continuum of sexual energy may reappear reciprocally as an excess of femininity in the sexuality of some men.* This is the case in some homosexual male personalities. Also, in some men the effect of the repression of female sexuality pushes them to a hypermasculinity (macho, chauvinist, etc), as they impose this repression both on women around them, and on the feminine qualities within themselves. Another devastating side effect of such repression is that many of the policies and attitudes adopted by feminist groups lead to the absorption of masculine tendencies and traits into the feminine personality, thus inhibiting the release of a long repressed femininity.

Dionysus: The Core of Feminine Sexuality

The unrepressed form of feminine sexuality is inexorably tied up with the notorious Greek god Dionysus, the god who was supposed to have given humanity the secrets of how to produce and use wine and all the merriment, drunkenness, suffering, and destruction associated with it. Dionysus was a woman's god and his celebrations were always initiated by women who would then bring men into the associated sacrificial rites and orgies. Research into the Dionysian tradition is fascinating for what it reveals about female sexuality and the reasons for the brutal repression of the principle of feminine sexuality in Western culture. Dionysian rites are based on a collective evocation of ecstatic states of mind through dance, drunkenness, music, chanting, sexual abandonment, hysteria, and pandemonium. *Ecstatic* literally means "a state of being outside oneself;" these ceremonies mark the religious forms in which Dionysus was considered the highest god. Dionysian religions or "mysteries" prevailed throughout the world prior to the formation of patriarchal male-dominated societies and are considered to be the repository of the most ancient Earth-Mother religions.

At the time of the winter sun, five days of ceremonies would begin with the cry of a sexually aroused bull, vocally pouring forth his primitive desires and terror into the black emptiness of the night. Women, aroused to frenzy with wine and whirling dance, would begin a nocturnal procession and rush impetuously into the night, swinging flaming torches in search of their life-giving god of death as he returned from his sojourn in the underworld. Early Dionysian ritual included animal sacrifice; during this ceremony, young goats were released before the procession. Women, be they maiden, matron or crone, ran after them with great speed and over great distance to capture, slay, and devour the raw flesh of these young animals. In this way, women snapped the ties with all the roles and responsibilities of birth-giving, nourishing and caring that enveloped their ordinary lives. Through Dionysian ritual, they descended into the primal, instinctual base of existence and symbolically filled themselves with the blood of the god who transforms life into death and death into life. At the same time, the men would retreat to the Temple of Apollo, the god of reason and conscious control. There, in solemn silence, they would refrain from drinking to contemplate the chalice full of wine and the empty satyr mask of terror, each a primary symbol of Dionysus.

In this ritual, men and women restore the primary reciprocity of their universal nature in the face of the paradoxical mystery of life: the male, like the sun, separates, comprehends, and illuminates the world from afar, the female energizes and vitalizes the earth from within.[29] When the procession ends, women with wine draw the men from the austerities of the temple into ecstatic ritual. At this stage the women, vibrant with guiltless lust, have absorbed some of the consciousness of the animals that were sacrificed. Animals possess a highly acute sense of perception and are aware of energies in nature that are undetectable to us. Because of this perceptual superiority, the gods in most ancient cultures were given animal form. It was believed intercourse with women in this ecstatic condition could transfer to the male this psychic, wordless level of perception.[30]

As seems to be the case in all successive periods of history, the qualities or things held in highest regard in one period become those most hated and despised in the following period. Thus, even as his rituals and aspects of his image were covertly adopted into the Christ story, Dionysus, in his lusty, erotic aspects, became in Christian theology Satan or the Devil. Let us examine the reasons behind this inversion and what it has meant to human sexuality.

Male-dominant patriarchal society, even in the crumbling phase we are experiencing now, is based on a dynamic that includes an excess of sanctimonious morality; dogmatic perfectionist imperatives upon which our work ethic, our career ambitions, and most of all our education systems are based. It is characteritzed as well by an unbending monolithic system of justice that takes into consideration no basic variations of human nature and applies an abstract standardized law to everyone. This standardization is extended to the realm of morality in which the enormously varied human psyches must submit to a ruthless standard of righteousness before a strict differentiation between Good and Evil. These patriarchal forms, which in recent generations we have labeled Puritanism and Victorianism, are still rampant beneath the progressive surface of modern lifestyles. They have extended covertly into the formulas of science and sociology and into political forms. Genetic engineering is a scientific attempt to eliminate defects and imperfection, illness, and even death, from the human genetic code. We are living under social and political ideologies that are hellbent on making the world a safe, comfortable, happy place, according to narrow formulas of elimination and exploitation. Under patriarchal theory, we as humans, both individually and collectively, are responsible for our own failures and miseries and it is our responsibility at any cost to eliminate those miseries. In sharp contrast to this stands the feminine, Dionysian form of religion and social order, which the patriarchy had to stamp out.

These mysterious feminine-dominant religions and social forms have been vanquished for so long that we have an almost total cultural amnesia concerning their view of reality. The importance of recapturing this viewpoint is clear. If the march of patriarchal rule continues, humanity may perish. Drawing upon scholarly works by Walter F. Otto, Edward C. Whitmont, and C. Kerenyi, I will summarize the meaning of Dionysian practices with an emphasis on their relevance to male/female sexuality in modern times..

Dionysian religion and ritual threatens the smugly comfortable and secure, systematized world of the patriarchal ideal, with a turbulent form of human behavior and belief. The call of Dionysus is a reminder to the well-ordered, routinized, domesticated world that a rupture and an unfathomable, terrifying unknowingness is the backdrop to our short lives on this Earth. An unknown, infinite black space surrounds our tiny sunlit planet: the primeval, endless cycles of time and the knowledge that all things from humans to stars are born, die, and constantly undergo transformation. Everything is constantly changing, to be finally devoured by time. As Hegel said, "It is the nature of the finite world to have within its essence the seeds of extinction, the hour of its birth is the hour of its death."[31]

Women, because they are so closely linked with the creative and generative processes of life, have a deep connection to this universal cycle. Women identify biologically with the universal decree that life and form must be destroyed in order to be reborn. Therefore, instinctually, they have an utterly different psychic connection to reality; the patriarchal view always seeks stability and an unchanging order. Dionysus, the god who is both ever-dying and ever-reborn, was the image through which women contacted this part of their innate reality. This contact was achieved through sexually induced ecstatic states in which all sense of ego and boundaries were lost; in which the individual allowed herself to be engulfed in a torrent of life that surges from the depths of her being. This ecstasy was a state in which the sense of life is intensified beyond the limits of self—a sense of life so strong that it could not perceive of its separation with death. The ecstatic state expressed the self-creating, self-destroying pulsation that is found at the very heart of life.

The Dionysian rituals allowed women to burst the bonds of marital duty and domestic custom in order to follow the torch of the god Dionysus over mountain tops and to fill the forests with wild shrieks of exultation. In this way, feminine sexuality went far beyond its relationship with men: it connected women with the sexual currents of nature and the earth. It was for these practices that women over four centuries were persecuted and burnt at the stake as witches. It is thus that women lost their important roles as priestesses, prophets, and magical healers.[32] One could say that modern discos, with their deafening pandemonious sound and whirling, flickering, blinding light effects, are a vulgar commercialized attempt to recapture the Dionysian ritual. Very often in discos it is the women who are moved to a greater excitement and release than the men.

The feminine psyche, through its Dionysian aspects, knows that the bond between opposites cannot be severed: there can be no light without darkness, there can be no joy without suffering. This idea was expressed beautifully in an Ingmar Bergman film, when Don Juan (the emissary of the Dionysian tradition) says to the devil: "I despise both God and Satan because they both pretend that good and evil are separate." The feminine consciousness understands this very well: that to create order, organization, and beauty, disciplines that subdue or control the powers of ugliness, darkness, and chaos are required. But in order to sustain these disciplines there must be ritual celebrations that release all those undesirable, unacceptable archetypal drives and emotional urges, which are necessarily part of the dual nature of the universe and of humans. This then is the nature of ritual: its symbolic impassioned rites transform the dark unwanted aspects of our personality integrating and channeling otherwise destructive urges. Ritual, which is also the origin of theater and religion, is the mechanism that prevents discipline from becoming repression.[33] We can see this function of ritual perverted and misunderstood in the violence and vulgarity of modern films and television, as well as in the public obsession with spectacle sports. Since both these forms of "modern entertainment" only display these violent fantasies, without allowing the purgative, controlled participation of the people in an actual, attuned, archetypal performance, they do not function as rituals. Patriarchal society, instead of using the combination of discipline and ritual to transmute this energy and establish order, uses such forces as religious piety, puritanism, rationality, ethics, good will, and common sense to quell the undesirable forces in human nature. When these means fail and the suppressed breaks forth, patriarchal society responds by imposing guilt, punishment, and a penal system.

Symmetry and Ritual

Dionysian ritual reflects a fundamental principle or law of nature that provides an epistomological key to understanding most matriarchal societies. That principle can be called the law of inversion. Mystical or ecstatic experiences, such as those triggered by Dionysian rites, provoke a heightened perception of the world. The dynamics of these forms of perception are now acknowledged, in theory, by modern physics. That is, the seemingly solid forms of our perceivable world are nothing more than minute, electro-magnetic wave patterns. Matter, at its base, is organized, symmetrically patterned vibrational energy. Practitioners of ecstatic rites through the centuries have reported visions of this pure energy that dances internally in symmetrical rhythmic patterns. Therefore, as the ancient Pythagorian philosophers believed, much about the fundamental nature of reality can be revealed by (1) the contemplation of pure symmetry and form or (2) the examination of a simple vibrating system.

On both of these levels of examination, we encounter the law of inversion. A symmetrical form is, in essence, a connection of opposites: top linked to bottom, left to right, outside to inside, front to back. Each one of these symmetrical oppositions is the inverse or mirror opposite of the other. The combining of inversed oppositions creates wholeness in geometric forms. The principle of oppositional inversion, which occurs spatially in symmetrical forms, occurs numerically, as time, in vibrational activity. For example, when a string of prescribed length and tension is struck, it vibrates at a specific frequency, let us say, one vibration per second. When one's finger allows only one half of that same string to vibrate, it will produce two vibrations per second, exactly twice the number of vibrations produced by striking its entire length. Likewise, when the string is held so that only one-third of it vibrates, it will produce three vibrations per second, or exactly three times that produced by striking its entire length. Therefore vibrations are connected to their generating source by numbers that are in an inverse relationship to one another.

This model will be used throughout the remainder of the book in a variety of contexts and analogies.

DIAGRAM 4. THE LAW OF INVERSION

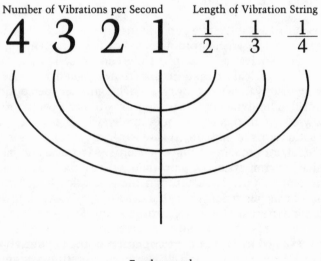

Number of Vibrations per Second

$$4 \quad 3 \quad 2 \quad 1$$

Length of Vibration String

$$\frac{1}{2} \quad \frac{1}{3} \quad \frac{1}{4}$$

Fundamental
Vibration

Between a vibrating frequency and its inverse lies an entire spectrum of either concordant or discordant vibratory possibilities. For example, one possible spectrum could be:

$$\frac{1}{2}, \ \frac{2}{3}, \ \frac{3}{4}, \ \mathbf{1}, \ \frac{4}{3}, \ \frac{3}{2}, \ \mathbf{2}$$

When inverse numbers are combined through multiplication (multiplication being the mathematical analogue of sexual intercourse), they create a unity or wholeness i.e., $\frac{3}{1} \times \frac{1}{3} = 1$. This process of crossing or multiplying oppositional inversions to obtain a unity is called reciprocity: one-third is the reciprocal of three. If we follow the metaphor of all ancient numerological philosophies, the number three corresponds with the Universal Male and the number two corresponds with the Universal Female.[34] It therefore follows that $\frac{3}{2}$ would represent the ideal balanced sexuality for a man, with the numerator three as his external masculine personality and two, the denominator, his internal female animus. With the same reasoning, the fraction $\frac{2}{3}$ can represent the ideal sexuality of a woman and $\frac{3}{2} \times \frac{2}{3} = 1$. *I propose that balance, harmony, and wholeness are achieved through this model of a fourfold reciprocity of opposites rather than the presently accepted concept of the equalization of differences.* The occurrence of the principle of reciprocity in ecstatic sexual union was described by Alan Watts:

> The two organs seem to change and change about in their roles so that the phallus becomes vulva, and vulva becomes phallus. Indeed, there exist Tibetan and Nepalese bronze images of this kind which, when separated, disclose the male with the vulva and the female with phallus. For there comes a strong physical experience of androgyny, of each sex completing and balancing itself by an infusion of the other. His urge and her surrender, his thrust and her opening, become a single feeling experienced equally in both. (*The Temple of Konarak: Erotic Spirituality*, p.90)

Reciprocity can be interpreted as a bonding between oppositional inversions and, as the myth inform us, Dionysus symbolizes the relational power that bonds opposites together and allows for a universe created from duality. Dionysus derives predominantly from the character of the Universal Feminine.

A simple perceptual experiment can allow one to experience the principle of inversion. When one stares into a bright green leaf intensely for a minute or two, one's eyes, in an inner vision, will see the opposite color on the spectrum, red. Scientific color theory states that a leaf appears to us as green because its molecules have absorbed all the red and orange wavelengths of color from the spectrum of natural light and reflect back to us only what remains: green. Our inner vision sees the inner, or absorbed, color of the leaf—red—while our external vision recognizes the leaf's green, material color quality. To experience the wholeness of the leaf requires the comprehension of both reciprocals, just as psychologically the comprehension of individuals requires an understanding of their absorbed or inner sexuality in relationship to their external sexuality.

Dionysian ritual enacts the cosmic interchange or reciprocity of inverse qualities:

> All life, all destruction, is immersed in the eternally circling rhythm of totality. Life becomes death and death becomes life, the human becomes godlike and the divine shows itself in human form, the animal takes unto itself spirit, and the hidden origin rises shining as the invisible goal. (Linda Fierz-David, *Women's Dionysian Initiation*, p. 30)

Women who refuse to relinquish their constant relational bond to family and children and abandon themselves to the worship of Dionysus were said to be cursed by the god in their motherhood so that consciously or unconsciously they would eventually destroy their own children.[35]

Mothering Practices and Femininity

In the absence of modern rituals that permit the expression of feminine sexuality, a fundamental imbalance occurs in all human sexuality. One cause of this imbalance is the repression in women of the reciprocal aspects of the yielding, mutable Universal feminine. Historically, men have been responsible for some of the vilest impositions of repression, both externally on women in the world and on the feminine principle within themselves. Equally significant, women continue to repress the feminine principle within themselves and in their offspring. Generally, the rearing of children is done by women, and so often competitive, aggressive, self-assertive qualities are fostered in boys and inhibited in girls. Girls are taught to be passive and yielding and are required to blunt their urges much more than boys. This became the almost uniformly accepted norm throughout the Christian world until as little as thirty years ago; a "good woman" does not have sexual feelings and urges at all.

In her book, *My Mother, My Self,* Nancy Friday traces the destructive repression of feminine sexuality that mothers exercise upon themselves and over their daughters and examines how this repression is propagated in a chain reaction generation after generation.[36] Once sexuality is repressed and unbalanced, there is a distortion or excess that appears elsewhere in the continuous connection between the feminine and the masculine. For centuries women have been programmed to believe that it is unacceptable for them to initiate sex with men or in any way be the seducer, the pursuer, or the instigator. Even in the so-called liberated climate of today, few women actually approach, invite, or initiate social or sexual engagements with men. To be a nice girl, the policy is still: "flirt a little and then wait and see". The programming of femininity into a role of passive neutrality shifts the entire responsibility for sexual advance onto men, thus overstimulating in them sexual assertion and aggression or, for some men, creating an inhibiting barrier that they find difficult to overcome. This leaves the more aggressive males an almost exclusive access to the more desirable women. Women, especially young girls, have until recently been programmed to believe that, in order to be considered decent, they literally have to resist sexual advances; when they are then "forced" or drugged into sex, they become "decent victims" of extenuating circumstance. Mothers typically convey this attitude of resistance to their daughters. Men, in response, confront this resistance with sexual persuasion. This deeply ingrained pattern of female resistance and male persuasion often persists into married life. Men are forced to think that they must be the seducers and, in the extreme, are given the psychological posture of a rapist. Part of the reason for "why men rape" lies in the excessive sexual passivity of women, a response that has been ingrained in them for generations. If the assertive, sexual, adventurous aspect of female sexuality were released, the pressures of male aggressiveness in

sexuality would probably diminish as well as the problem of
female rape.

The repression of these aspects of the feminine by the mother
figure, as recounted in the myth of Parsifal, is alive today. The
maternal component of femininity is instinctively sexually repressive. It is the maternal that must divert the Oedipal tendencies of the child, especially those of the male, away from herself.
So normally a woman instinctively divests herself of sexual allure and projection with her children, especially during their
sensitive sexual formation. The maternal figure in our society
does this by creating a puritan or virginal image of herself. Some
men never survive this image and adopt the mother/whore di-
chotomy in their subconscious attitude toward all women. This
syndrome can be described as an unconscious attitude that any
sexual woman is an oversexed woman, "not pure like Mom."
This attitude, projected onto all women, creates in men a crush-
ing puritanical treatment of feminine sexuality, including the
feminine within himself.

Why, may we ask, in Western psychology, does the mother
image act upon her children, as in the Oedipus myth, as either
a repressive or distorting force? One of the most convincing
responses is given by Jean Liedloff in her book, *The Continuum
Concept,* Ms. Liedloff lived in the Venezuelan jungle with Stone
Age Indian tribes, and there she recognized the enormous change
that the mother/child relationship had undergone in the transition from Stone Age matriarchal societies to industrial patriarchal societies. She describes how, among these tribes, the child
is placed at the moment of birth in the mother's arms. It remains
in constant physical contact with the mother for six to eight
months thereafter. The child is never denied the warmth of the
mother's body, or the sound of her heartbeat. During that entire
period the child experiences the whole spectrum of the mother's
busy physical life. Working, eating, sleeping, excreting—the continuum between child and mother is not broken. By contrast,
Western civilization sets up an immediate cycle of alienation,
loneliness, and fear by snatching the new born infant away from
its mother, placing it into the hands of the doctors and nurses,
and then enclosing and isolating it in cribs, playpens and empty
rooms.

> We are disengaged from our human continuum at
> birth, left starving for experience in cots and prams,
> away from the stream of life. Part of us remains
> infantile and cannot contribute positively to our lives

as older children and adults. But we do not, we
cannot, leave them behind. The want of in-arms
experience remains alongside the development of
mind and body, waiting to be fulfilled.

We in civilization share certain ailments of the
continuum. Self-hate and self-doubt are quite general
among us, in varying degrees, depending upon how
and when the complex of deprivations affected our
inherited qualities. The quest for in-arms experience,
as the years pass and we grow up, takes on a great
many forms. Loss of the essential condition of well
being that should grow out of one's time in arms
leads to searches and substitutions for it. *Happiness
ceases to be a normal condition of being alive, and
becomes a goal.* The goal is pursued in short- and
long-term ways. (p. 114)

The patriarchal impulse in history has won out and separated the infant from a continuous flow of love and intimacy
with the mother. The human psyche always yearns for the eternal protective love to usher it into life. If it is fulfilled at that
time, we are freed, but if it is denied we men become, like Oedipus, unconsciously dominated by our yearning for our mother.

Once again, we can look to tribal cultures for grounds to
enable us to view the complex "mother problem" which haunts
the psychology of this patriarchal age. The Earth-Mother cultures, almost universally, followed the relational pattern outlined by Liedloff—during infancy and early childhood, the child
is saturated by a constant physical relationship with the mother
but then, somewhere between eight and fourteen years of age,
the male leaves the mother permanently. Separated from her
field of influence, he enters male society and male initiations.
He first has sexual initiations and receives an education that
includes, at least in several known traditions, a degree of control
over his sexual emissions. These are followed by vocational,
spiritual, and cosmological initiations, all of which strengthen
his masculine identity. Modern men have no such initiatory
stages of development. They move from the influence of the
mother to the influence of the archetype of the Armored Knight
that, in reality, remains a "mother-pleasing" phase of development.

Mothering practices, like sexual practices, become formalized in a society. All forms come into existence through the law
of duality. Any form manifests a set of characteristics (i.e.,

round, red, hard) while all oppositional characteristics (i.e., flat, green, soft) remain repressed. All processes of growth and transformation begin with a release of the repressed, oppositional characteristics, which initially act negatively and adversely upon the existing established characteristics. The established resists, and this resistance constitutes the second phase of the transformational process. The third phase is the manifestation of the positive aspect of the repressed quality. We can observe this same triadic universal law in the repression/release cycle of the feminine and the maternal. Generations raised after the late 1960's, early 1970's, already began to escape the powerful negative influence of the sexually repressive mother. Because married women were drawn into the work force, children raised after these threshold years were actually starved for any motherly influence in their development, positive or negative. Children of working mothers today are often nurtured and controlled by frozen dinners and T.V. hypnotics. This constitutes the second phase in which the negative repressive characteristics of motherhood are blocked and nullified. Sexual repression follows the same pattern:

Phase 1 Repression/Release: pornography, promiscuity, indulgence, illness

Phase 2 Resistance: the new conservatism, fundamentalism

Phase 3 Re-emergence: an integrated sexuality may evolve that is the complement to the past patriarchal form.

The present repressed state of femininity is almost the inverse, or opposite, of how female energy would manifest in a society that held femininity in highest esteem. In earlier matriarchal cultures, masculine characteristics were given a secondary value by both men and women; this emphasis on the feminine radically affected sexuality, on both a social and an individual level. Let us examine next how a reemergence of female sexuality may evolve.

8·

Matriarchy: Reemergence of Female Sexuality

The feminine Dionysian ritual aimed toward an ecstatic reunion with the maternal source of our being, a source that houses the most powerful instincts of our nature—sexuality, aggression, and fear—and binds them inseparably. Aggression, like love and sexuality, is indispensable for the development and functioning of the individual ego. Just as the individual must struggle through the birth canal in order to enter the world, so too we must confront conflicts, assert our will, and strengthen our self-confidence in order to love and relate fully. In brief, self-definition occurs through struggle. Aggression and acquisitiveness are praised in the business and professional world, just as they are in national politics and sports. To quote Edward Whitmont:

> The social regulation of aggression demands both
> expression and inhibition . . . in order to personalize
> violence and taste the possibility of victory in
> aggression, there must also be an object to be
> vanquished. The psychology of the personalizing of
> violence through aggression expresses the fact that
> victimization and submission demand to be
> experienced actively but also passively. (*Return of the
> Goddess*, p.19)

We enjoy conflict in the sports arena, but we have a double standard for this reality in our social and sexual roles. The joy and relief that come with aggressively breaking down unwanted structures are prohibited in our ethical attitudes, as is much of the natural expression of anger, rage, and destruction. We are trained to believe that these qualities in our nature are socially impermissible and wrong, so moral repressions mount to dangerously explosive levels. Moreover, our society even finds unacceptable the processes of aggression and destruction within our own psyches, as, for example, when old personality structures dissolve to make way for new emerging aspects of ourselves. These natural breakdowns and changes in internal processes often conflict with our rigid social institutions, resulting in divorce, nervous breakdowns, abandoned careers, etc. None of these have a way of expressing themselves positively in our rigid, patriarchal society. Once again, we find social institutions in conflict with the psychological nature of man.

In human physiology, the neural pathways of aggression and erotic sexuality are interrelated in the lower brainstem. Aggression and sexuality are instinctive archetypal reactions that are irresistible and interwoven. The desire of a man to penetrate a woman, whether out of anger and aggression or erotic passion, reveals the same need: a greater involvement.[37] We discover here a concurrence of opposites: with the subjugation of aggression comes also diminishment of sexual passion, a diminution that obscures the spiritual potentialities of sexuality, with explosive negative results in both drives.

There is a threshold of heightened pleasure that, when crossed, creates a mindless yearning for its own opposite—pain and self-destruction. The beloved, within the envelope of erotic passion, feels so defenseless and completely surrendered to the lover that the idea of death can feel imminent and even desirable. One Tantric text states, "the surrender of love is a transcendental death."[38] The inverse dynamic has been reported by the people who have been attacked by large carnivorous animals. David Livingstone's famous account describes how the pain and fear within him, caused by a lion's claws and teeth, transmuted into a pleasant, peaceful sensation, while the animal was attempting to devour him. The same chemicals associated with sexual abandonment are released at the time of death or near-death.

Feminine power has its dark side just as certainly as does masculine power: it can be stagnating, stifling, and depressively oppressive. A newspaper article from Madrid shows its reemergence: "Police believe a man who claims he was raped at gun point may have been the victim of lesbian extremists . . . [he] was bundled into a car . . . by two women as he walked along a Madrid street. He was subjected to a half-hour sex ordeal. Doctors said the man was assaulted with an elongated vegetable."[39] In the balance of nature, the positive aspect of feminine aggression and sexuality naturally emerge as a response to the excesses of male patriarchal oppression. However, this shift will have to be guided by women, who are consciously aware of the complexities of the vast transition humanity is undergoing.

There can also be positive results from the inverse bonding between aggression and sexual attraction, between death and love. In some cases, a deep, fulfilled expression of one's sexuality can either reduce the tendency toward aggression or give the feelings of anger and aggression a clarity and balance that is creative and not clouded or distorted by repressions. Individuals who have been fortunate enough to have experienced a deep, fulfilling love are often more accepting and positive about their own death.

Spanish culture maintains a ritual tradition based on the mysterious connection between love and death. The matador is an image of the force of love that must confront and master, not only death, but also the fear of death. The superb contemporary Spanish film, *Matador*, by Alnovonar, explores the nuances of this legacy from the ancient Dionysian tradition. In the Spanish world, there are two forms of bull fighting: one in which the matador battles the bull to exhaustion, the other in which the bull must be killed. Alnovonar alludes to the idea that the matador is the symbol of the animus (the male component within the female psyche), which explains the feminine allure in the matador's costume. The bull is raw, primal, male sexual energy—it is the animus, the masculine aspect in the woman that has the potential of either mastering and subduing the primal masculine force, or destroying it. As we pass through the transition leading to the ascendency of the feminine, we must be aware of the destructive effect militant feminism can have on the masculine during this vulnerable period.

Alnovonar also explores the mysterious relationship between death and orgasm. In French the male orgasm is called *la petite mort*, ("the little death"). The bodily surrender that must be made to achieve a full sexual climax is the same surrender that the body must make to death. As with the Dionysian revelation, love, life, and death merge in orgasm. Hence a great knowledge is required to obtain (a desired response) from this profound bodily explosion.

Modern science is now coming forth, with its cold rational form of evidence, to support a tug of war between love and death. More and more, research shows the positive effect that sexual fulfillment, loving, and being loved has on the immune system.[40] Our ability to naturally protect ourselves from disease is completely bound up with chemical and hormonal changes in the body related to the experience of love and sexual expression. Reichian therapy has accumulated a great deal of clinical information on how the blockage of sexual and emotional energy creates conditions that contribute to cancer, arthritis, and heart trouble. Added to this, the great killer in the Western world, substance abuse, is extensively linked to the denial, alienation, and deprivation of sexuality and emotion in one's life. The mounting evidence is so strong that we can almost say that most humans die from a lack of love—there is no greater "natural cause" of death. Our society, in this period, so limits the full giving and receiving of love and the full expression of sexuality that we are falling under the domination of love's adversary, death.

Both male and female energies must be proportionately adjusted to reflect the universal balance between sexuality and aggression, between love and death. Women need to become more familiar with their levels of aggression, to learn to use and transform them into real tools for empowerment. Men need to reduce aggressive competitiveness and to learn to accept in themselves fear, the experience of failure, and the surrender and receptivity necessary to give and receive love and sexual pleasure. The need for rebalancing explains, in part, the emphasis on the release of female aggressiveness as part of the reemergence of female sexuality. The fundamental nature of femininity is receptive, yielding, nourishing, giving, weak, soft, and mutable. But, by the "law of opposites," there must also be an equal power of opposite strength in order to permit and protect that extreme helplessness. This range of qualities can be seen in nature by observing a female bird and her young chicks in the nest. The female bird is totally self-sacrificing, building and securing a nest, searching and delivering food, mouthful after mouthful, to a brood of hungry young. But when a threatening predator approaches the nest, this all-yielding mother turns into an aggressive demon—attacking with an unrestrained cruelty and vengeance far exceeding male aggressive patterns, which are often linked to ritual mating and territorial performance. To touch, caress, and fondle involves the same action as to strike and inflict pain, it is only a difference in degree or intensity. The release of female love and sexuality must include its polar opposite, the release of unmitigated power.

In mythology, the goddess who embodies the aggressive aspect of femininity is Diana or Artemis, the Amazon warrior woman. Artemis is *not* modeled on the male hero warrior. She is the aggressive, protecting quality within the feminine itself. I feel it is the Artemis image that women now need to discover, instead of attempting to imitate the masculine warrior model, with its ritual aggression and competition, suitable for the world of sports, business, and politics. The woman warrior impulse is not a demonstration of strength against strength; it is not the rule of the victor over the vanquished; it is not the test-and-trial-by-conflict that is basic to the organization of male society. On the contrary, this form of female aggression is associated with the violent response that arises to protect all that is weak, helpless, dark, and hidden. This is a quality that both men and women must learn to use and express. Men regain for themselves, in releasing the principle of female sexuality—including the dark and destructive—a most significant role. They will redeem, through male reason and symbolic knowledge, the constructive aspects of female aggression, which are often immersed in an indistinguishable sea of emotions and feeling. Through the priestess-warrior Artemis, women and men will find the necessary course of action to protect the sick and dying Earth Mother, Gaia. It is only through the feminine warrior, the protectoress of the sacred value of the Earth, that the destructive exploitation of our planet by a degenerating patriarchal society can be impeded. This form of female aggressiveness, if unrepressed, would not tolerate the vile ugliness and destruction that the patriarchal industrial world has perpetrated on the natural environment.

Women, more or less consciously, are seeking to discover this Artemis image of themselves in gymnasiums, sporting events, and fitness programs around the world. The American Association for the Advancement of Science reports that athletic women cut their risk of breast and uterine cancer in half and the most common form of diabetes by two-thirds. Time Magazine, citing Harvard reproductive biologist Rose Frisch who led a study of 5,398 women, reports that:

The long term effects of early exercise on health are impressive. Exercise shuts down the production of certain reproductive hormones in women. Vigorous training can temporarily lengthen or even eliminate a runner's menstrual cycle . . . active women produce a less potent form of estrogen than their sedentary counterparts. Result: breast and uterine tumors that depend on the hormone cannot develop as easily. In addition, athletes lack excess body fat, which can predispose people to diabetes. Frisch cautions that low estrogen levels can lead to temporary infertility.[41]

This scientific information contains an important support for a main premise in this book: women, through physical discipline, are changing the balance and quality of sexual energies in their own bodies. The muscles, the hormones, the metabolism are responding to different archetypal energies. The universal mothering principle, Demeter, is giving ground to Artemis, the independent warrior. I believe that men must follow this lead and also discover physical and psychological disciplines that will broaden the archetypal identities of masculinity, as well as change the internal processes of their bodies.

Toward a Balanced Society

The patriarchal mind cannot fathom the paradoxical relationship that exists between all opposites, such as darkness and light, death and life, aggression and love, hence repressive inhibitions are placed upon individuals and society alike. Psychologist Anthony Storr describes the dangerous by-products that result from inhibiting human aggression:

> The tendency is for a paranoid projection: that is ascribing one's undesirable aggressive traits to another; the invention of artificial weapons that depersonalize combat and prevent face to face an encounter with the enemy as vulnerable human beings; the aggregation into larger societies which submerges individuality; the effects upon hostility of crowding. . . . All these trends increase the danger that our aggressive impulses cannot be adequately integrated into social functioning. Thus we must face the alarming fact that present day man, unlike the animal, cannot rely upon the automatic functioning of instinctive aggressive inhibition. (*Return of the Goddess*, p.26)

This danger, more than anything, signals the need for the return of feminine qualities as a dominant element in human psychology. There is no quality, there is no behavior, there is no human experience, that does not have both a positive and a negative aspect. This includes aggression, rape, child sexuality, rage, and anger. When a society labels certain aspects of human experience and human nature as unacceptable, there must be a symbolic ritualistic practice through which the emotions beneath these experiences can be discharged safely and transformed. The key to uncovering new forms of ritual lie, as always, in a deeper understanding of human sexuality. But for the time being this new awareness is frightening and often misunderstood by the crumbling patriarchal mentality.

The past two millennia of patriarchal society have encouraged the development of a sense of individual ego. Each person can identify himself or herself as a separate entity, self-motivated and self-controlled. Exposure to ancient metaphysical philosophies has begun to offset this self-image and allows us to understand ourselves as instruments of the powerful universal and natural forces that flow through our being, moving and controlling us. The sense of individuality has been a great prize, one which perhaps only the patriarchal formula could procure as an experience of consciousness. But the price of alienation from one another, nature, and our planet is now becoming life threatening. The entire premise underlying modern psychology will be altered as the repression of the feminine is released during the declining phase of patriarchy. Modern psychology believes the brain/mind to be the generator of the moods, emotions, reactions, feeling, and behavior in general, of the individual. But the feminine, Dionysian perception is that the brain is not a generator but a receiving station for emotional and mental energies that exist in fields of consciousness surrounding all of matter. An innovative psychologist, Liz Greene, with a doctorate degree in Jungian psychology, uses the ancient metaphor of astrology to explain the human psyche. She uses an integrating model, one in which there is an interaction between the universal energy and the interior of each person. Human behavior is, in astrology, modified by the positions of planets, stars, the sun, and the moon.[42] This model is not dissimilar to those found in the modern science of bioclocks. Whether the theory of astrology is ultimately sound or not is not really the point here. What is of interest is a paradigm that creates a sense of unity between man and the environment, between the earth and the heavens. The continuing increase of popular and scientific interest in astrology can be seen as part of the emerging matriarchy's intuitive and integrating consciousness.

The sun, the moon, and the planets, in ancient philosophies, have the same attributes as the major archetypal patterns of the human psyche. Mars equals aggression and physical force; Venus, sensual allure and intrigue. These and other ways of conceiving analogies between internal and external experience can allow each individual to acknowledge a continuous interrelationship of his psyche with that of universal nature. This will ultimately help us to liberate ourselves from the ego-centered and guilt-ridden psychology of today. The scientific evidence supporting this and other paradigms is growing. What needs to change is the way we think about the wealth of information science has and is divulging. I believe that mental processes in the intuitive, connecting analogical mode, characteristic of the universal feminine intelligence, will play a major role in scientific method of the future.

Even materialistic, rational science requires the presence of an invisible world to explain reality. The invisible physical universe of science is polarized: gravity/radiation, magnetism/electricity. Our sexuality also connects us to an invisible world of archetypal energy, psychic patterns, and stereotypes. We can, as individuals, balance, control, cultivate, and direct our sexuality so that it is in tune with, and contributes to, the vast changes occurring within human society and the natural world. We cannot superimpose the dream of matriarchy upon our presently disturbed and polluted environment, but we can, through the intensity of our imagination and our sexuality, plant the seeds of change for the future.

III·

SEXUALITY AND SOCIETY

ROADMAP: DREAMING
THE CREATION

The fundamental difference between our modern technological society and such societies as those of Ancient India and
Egypt, as well as most tribal societies, is that ours is predominantly economic and materialistic, whereas ancient societies
were founded upon a spiritual or religious reality, around which
material life was organized. When we attempt to conceive of the
path history will take for the future of human society, we can
use several graphic images or time lines. History may be travel-
ing in a straight line, which would indicate an extension of technological growth and development. Our future, as our present,
may be dominated by evermore complex scientific advancements, technological innovations, and vast governmental and
military institutions. On the other hand, history may, like the
curvature of universal space in modern physics, travel in a circle
or a spiral. The beginning point of a circular path is the same
as its end. The future, therefore, may advance us toward a return
to our origins, similar to some primary state, yet transfigured
by the experience of time.

The discussion of sexuality and society that follows is based
on a circular or spiraling view of the movement of history. I will
use images and patterns of the past not as recipes, or as models to
be copied, but as a means of stimulating imaginings of possible
futures.

In Part 2, I explored some of the original connections between sexuality and the spiritual. I will discuss, in this section,
the connection of these two to the third element of our triad,
to society. In the past, societies have been based on either spirituality, or religion, or both. Religion and spirituality both use
ritual as a means of perpetuating the underlying reality and ob-
jectives of our society. In spiritually oriented rituals, human

contact and exchange occurs with the invisible energies that pervade the world. Religious ritual, as I define it, differs from spiritual ritual in it, the ethics, laws, and decrees, through which the individual maintains a responsible relationship to the physical world and society, are reinforced.

Ritual society recognizes that there is a division at the core of existence. To the Australian Aborigines, who have the oldest continuous ritual-based culture known, on one "side" are the extraordinary, invisible powers that have created and laid down the plan of life. Humans cannot ordinarily experience those powers, which have withdrawn to the interior being of earth and sky and are indwelling throughout all of creation. In order for humanity to live in harmony and balance, we must maintain a constant communication with these extraordinary powers, so that human behavior and social structures can conform to their metaphysical laws. According to the Aboriginal culture, the powers originally created the world plan by dreaming: they believe that the great ancestor (an archetypal being) first conceived his objectification while sleeping. He visualized his travels— the countryside, the songs, and everything in creation that he makes—inside his head, before they were externalized. All objects of nature are conceived as external projections of internal visions.[1] Everything comes to the material world from the inner visions of the great ancestor while in a dream or ecstatic state. Through ritual, humans can recapture, and identify with, the original world-creating "dreaming" of the ancestor. New songs, dances, rites, and magical abilities can be conferred on people who are in special psychic or ecstatic states. This level of Aboriginal ritual enactment is similar to sexuality, in that both require an intensification of bodily and emotional energy, which lift one's awareness beyond mundane conditioning.

9·

Functions of Ritual

Ritual has been used by societies for two main purposes: one may be called creative and the other integrative. The creative function, as among Australian Aborigines, has the purpose of maintaining harmony and balance between humanity, society, and nature. In addition to this creative aspect, the intense human impulses that threaten the norms and ethos of society are rechanneled through the cathartic effects of ritual release. In other words, ritual allows an integration of the unwanted, antisocial aspects of human nature. In modern Jungian psychology, these dark, unwanted aspects are referred to as the shadow component. This "inferior" side or shadow of human nature may be regarded as a symbol for all that is base, unformed, and unconscious within the individual. It pertains to parent images and to identification with events of the distant past.

Jung called this shadow a moral problem that challenges the whole ego-personality, for no one can become conscious of the shadow without considerable moral effort. To become conscious of it involves recognizing dark aspects of the personality as present and real. This act is the essential condition for any kind of self-knowledge.[2]

Instead of the repression of our shadowy side, ritual allows for its transformation and release. But the archaic form of release is based on a state of being that has been subsumed in the cosmic spiral of evoluntionary consciousness. In the preceding feminine/mythic society, the clan, the tribe, the collective mentality, existed as a single organism; in other words the group consciousness existed as one individual. We now have a highly

individualized identity that inhibits the depth of empathy required for a true ritual release.

Ritual and Sexuality: Taboos and Releases

Every aspect of human nature that is repressed, ignored, or denied arises again in its dark, perverted, and toxic form. Every
behavior that people carry out, including the most vile and unwanted, is an aspect of all our natures and cannot be repressed
without immediate or eventual destructive consequences. The
perverse, the dark, the lustful, wells up around us, erupting in
wars, psychotic slaughters and crimes, the destructive and self-
destructive patterns of populations. We celebrate our holidays
with a bloodbath of highway death tolls. These attitudes threaten
to finally engulf the facade of peace, stability, and permanency.
In earlier societies, through ritual enactment, unacceptable aspects of human nature were integrated with the positive. Some
psychologists, including Freud, have understood this significance
of ritual for nearly a century. We must find a means of applying
ritual enactments in our world before we collapse in a cataclys-
mic reaction to centuries of repression. To contrast our repressive techniques of social order with those more integrated
methods of past societies, let me cite some examples.

It is well understood that children have strong sexual drives
and needs, which our society pretends are non-existent. But in,
for example, ancient Chinese culture, children were usually encouraged to be present in the bed chambers of their older sisters,
brothers, or cousins during their sexual dalliances and lovemaking. The children were also given male and female dolls with
obvious sex organs (unlike the castrated Barbie and Ken) allowing
them to become playfully familiar with genitals and their use.[3]
Patriarchy and puritanism has, for centuries, blocked the playful
touching and sexual affections between adults and children, so
common and natural in older societies. The result of this repression is that our society drowns in an ever-mounting exposé of
horrific child abuse, child rape, child prostitution, and crimes of
exploitation.

Freudian psychology has acknowledged a sexual component
in parent/child relationships, that there are sexual attractions
between mothers and sons and fathers and daughters. A positive
appreciation on the part of the parent for their children of the
opposite sex is indeed necessary for the psychological develop-

ment of the child. But with our taboos, the overt acknowledgement of these attractions is prohibited. As a result, the repressed
attachment between parents and their children of the opposite
sex can remain into adulthood, often with paralytic effects on
the mature sexual relationships of the children. A striking contrast to our repression of this parent/child dynamic was found in
ancient North African societies. Here the father took the virginity of each of his daughters on the night just before the young
girl was to marry. On this one and only occasion the father, under
the supervision of the priest, introduced his daughter to her
sexual life in a ritual sexual ceremony.[4] Of course, from our
point of view, this is an extreme and undesirable practice, but
theoretically one can see the possible value of this custom in
that the father certainly should be sexually knowledgeable and
full of tenderness and care for his daughter's important and sensitive initiation. At the same time, the practice could release all
the accumulated subliminal attractions that often exist between
youth and parent. Certainly, this seems a primitive approach,
but is it any more primitive than the ritual of countless modern
young girls who painfully lose their virginity in the back of a
panel van in the hands of an ill-prepared, often aggressive, and
drunken young boyfriend?

Another taboo in our society is hetero-oral sex, which only
a couple of hundred years ago in France was punishable by exile
or death. Although this practice has recently gained a certain
conversational popularity, it remains for many on the lewd or
unacceptable list. In ancient societies the courtesans, female
temple dancers and musicians, and all women associated with
the erotic arts had a tradition in which those who had become
masters in the art of oral sex painted their lips bright red to
celebrate and advertise their achievement.[5] Very few modern
women are aware that this is the origin and significance of wear-
ing lipstick. Cleopatra, as reported by the Greek historian Herodotus, was celebrated throughout the world for her mastery in this
science of pleasure. How different is this behavior surrounding
sexuality, even from present day so-called liberated attitudes.

In Greek mythology, Medea kills the children she loves to
punish the husband she loves, because he rejects her. The myth
describes the paradox contained in the principle of motherhood:
the maternal instinct sacrifices and struggles always for the birth,
protection, and nourishment of life. At the same time the universal mother, or Mother Earth, who gives birth to all things, eventually and unceasingly destroys everything that is born.

The paradoxical light and dark sides of motherhood are also

portrayed symbolically by the two leading female roles in the modern film *Fatal Attraction*. The male lead, played by Michael Douglas, is a striving, performing, patriarchal yuppie business- man caught between these polarities. The film opens with an atmospheric description of the humdrum contentments and mi- nor upsets of normal domestic bourgeois life. His wife is sweet and giving, but intensity and romance are always side-stepped in order to serve the family's needs. Douglas, through his slick business world, meets the modern, single career girl. While his wife is away visiting the grandparents, he slips into a one-night- stand sexual encounter. More encounters follow; they rage with dark, violent passions and a depth of eroticism that Douglas has never experienced in his married life. In the story line, Glenn Close becomes obsessed with Douglas and wants to possess him as her own. Although her role begins as the red-hot, one-night- stand lover, she quickly transforms into the role of the rejected and dark mother. Even though they only had a few sexual epi- sodes, she claims that she is pregnant and wants to be the mother of Douglas' child. The story line soon becomes only a thin facade, covering the reality that Close's obsessive behavior is an expres- sion of the characteristics of the universal dark mother. It be- comes evident that Close, like Medea, is willing to destroy herself, her lover, as well as her own fetal child. Ironically, she's capable of killing the man who is the object of her obsession, as well as his wife who represents the positive maternal instinct. Throughout the film, particularly in the sexual scenes, water is used symbolically, as it is in many myths, to represent the stir- ring of the deep subconscious layers. In the final scene, Douglas tries to destroy Close by drowning her in a bathtub, symbolizing his attempt to force the dark passionate element of his own psyche back into the confines of his subconscious. But, as in the film, men alone do not have the power to control and repress these subconscious feminine forces. Close rises from the waters of the tub, enraged, uncontrollably psychotic, to destroy again. *Fatal Attraction* ends with the wife shooting the dark feminine character through the heart, thus saving her domestic male. They both return to the dull normalcy of their bourgeois life.

The world condition tells us that our fatal attraction to the dark passions of the subconscious can no longer be contained or repressed by the busy, successful industriousness and domestic- ity of middle class life. Disturbing social conditions announce that society must find the psychology and social institutions that allow for the wholeness and integration of both the polarities of our nature. Those discoveries must somehow be involved with the rebirth and new understanding of ritual.

Ritual and Balance of Sexual Energy

As we have stated, ritual has constructive uses other than the release of the negative aspects of our psyche. One of those is to maintain a balance between masculine and female energies. For example, when a social code necessitates that a person respond consistently to a particular pattern, he or she at the same time denies the existence of the opposite portion of that pattern. If you are trained to externalize one half of your total pattern, it is inevitable that the seeds of your other half are sown somewhere in your internal being and need some form of expression. If, as so often is the case, men and women are trained by society into a dominant and submissive pattern (because that fulfills organizational demands, as well as responds to the archetypal characteristics of masculinity and femininity), then a balancing of the hidden element through ritual is demanded.

Morris Berman cites a study by Gregory Bateson in which he described how a tribal Balinese Iatmil society maintained its balance of male/female energies through ritual:

> Every society must develop a separate ethos for maleness and for femaleness. Even here, men must be performers, (in the Iatmil society the male functions mostly theatrically and in ritualized hunting, etc.). They must be competitive, aggressive, dominant and more destructive, etc. (all the characteristics we now criticize in men). The females in this society normally assume an opposite or complementary role. The difference between our society and the tribal is that the tensions which develop from these dynamic oppositions are relieved frequently through a Ritual enactment called a "Naven" (similar to our idea of theatre). In this ceremony each sex is allowed to be the other and sometimes the women wear dildos and the men dress as women. The women act out domineering aggression over the men and ritually copulate the helpless submissive men. (All of this is performed in heightened ecstatic states.) (*The Reenchantment of the World*, p.43)

The most accessible ritual available to us is ritual sexuality, and the reversal of the dominance/submissive pattern is perhaps, symbolically, the most important function of ritual. *The question that faces us is, how we can return to the ritual power of sexuality a ritual that would allow us to purify of the inseparable dark aspects of human nature, without regressing to a pre-individualized state of consciousness?*

10·

Orgasm, Ritual, and Society

The reversal of the dominance/submissive pattern can be translated from the ancient tribal mode to modern individualized men and women. This form of ritualized sexuality is dependent upon the male achieving the ability to control his ejaculation and/or retain his spermatic fluid. Once capable of this, a modern couple can achieve a reversal of physiological roles. The withholding of the male orgasm creates such an intensification of passions that the archetypal energies of ritual can enter the couple. In this state, the female partner can vividly imagine that the penis is now a part of her and she can become fully assertive and dominant in sexual activity. This role reversal based on ejaculation control is the doorway to an entire theater, in which heightened passion allows the couple to unfold all the fantasized archetypal roles embedded in the human subconscious.

Techniques to Control Ejaculation

An idea that surprises most men is that orgasm and ejaculation are two distinctly different bodily responses. Because we were not trained to control our ejaculation in early adolescence, it seems at first to be unnatural and to require some effort. The methods involved with separating orgasmic response from ejaculaton begin with controlling a specific muscle, the pubococcygens muscle (P.C.), in a way that is not very different from training and developing one's biceps. The P.C. muscle transverses the perineum area of the torso, which in men is from the base of the testicles to the anus. This deep muscular region is the foundation of the torso, and functions both consciously and unconsciously to maintain continence of the anus and genitals.

One can easily become aware of this muscle's function while urinating. Muscle contraction interrupts the flow of urine, while its relaxation allows the urine to flow again. The function of the P.C. muscle can be extended to control and prevent seminal emission during orgasm. Even preliminary experimentation indicates that a conscious, definite contraction near the threshold of orgasm can block the ejaculation response and that with continued practice and effort this control can be more or less stabilized. A number of changes in attitude about sexuality from both partners are necessary to make this practice successful. But if the awareness and desire is there, its employment can open up an entirely new level of sexual experience for both partners.

Men can use various methods to gain this control, such as: (1) drawing up of the P.C. muscle and exerting a pumping action; (2) applying firm pressure to the prostate area during intercourse; (3) breathing deeply with emphasis on inhalation; and (4) changing the mental focus or attention. Any combination of the above can be used in lovemaking, particularly during the climb toward climax to delay or avoid ejaculation.

A certain amount of information needs to be acquired about the effects and side effects of this practice. The gland in the male system that is strongly affected by these methods is the prostate gland, which absorbs and collects the semen manufactured in the testicles before it descends into the penis for ejaculation. The principle consistent in all these methods, be they Taoist from China, or Tantric from India, is that the semen is held in reserve in the prostate and can from there be reabsorbed into the blood. The vital (male) hormones, enzymes, nutrients, and amino acids are thus returned to the system. To prevent stagnation and painful congestion in the prostate region, it is necessary first to practice certain deep breathing methods and then to learn how to rhythmically and forcefully contract the P.C. muscle, which in turn massages and stimulates the prostate. Manual massage of that region is required daily and especially at intervals during sexual intercourse. These practices assist in releasing the spermatic essence from the gland into the bloodstream. To achieve this goal, daily breathing practice, contraction of the P.C. muscle, and prostatic massage are to be done like a calisthenic. Some books recommend two sessions of at least seventy-five contractions per day, in addition to interim practice during intercourse itself. The inconvenience of this discipline is very slight because this calisthenic can be practiced almost anywhere, during normal daily activities. It is important to adjust the practice of these disciplines to a level that is appropriate to one's requirements in life.[6]

The goal put forward by the more spiritually oriented books on this subject is that the male should never ejaculate for the rest of his life. Complete elimination of ejaculation, if done correctly along with certain meditation techniques, is supposed to yield miraculous spiritual and physical advances. While this may be the case, there is also a range of more realistic alternatives, such as those recommended in *Sexual Energy Ecstasy* by David Alan Ramsdale and Ellen Jo Dorfman. This book recommends that each man find his own personal rhythm of voluntary ejaculation. In other words, there is a certain number of days after a man has had an ejaculation during which there is a build up toward the time when another ejaculation becomes imperative. That is when an orgasm has to be released, either through compulsive masturbation or a wet dream. Each man should discover his own rhythm and, during those days, whether it is three or four days or more, have sexual intercourse without ejaculation. This allows for a reserve of spermatic fluids to build up in the prostate, with a portion of that fluid being reabsorbed into the system. Once voluntary ejaculation is allowed, the blocking contraction method is again applied during the orgasm, with the optimum effect being that only a built up reserve of sperm escapes, rather than an emission that depletes the system of nutrients and hormones.[7]

In addition to finding a personal rhythm for voluntary ejaculation as a means of seminal conservation, various books, particularly ancient texts, give fixed formulas. One Chinese text recommends that a man make love very frequently, but emit only two or three times for every ten coitions. Another, *The Secret of the Jade Bedroom*, makes a recommendation according to a man's age:

Vigorously healthy males at 15 years can ejaculate twice a day, at 30 once a day, at 40 once in three days, at 50 once every five days, at 60 once every ten days and at 70 once every thirty days. Unhealthy males should wait twice as long between emissions for example, at 30 years once every two days. (*Sexual Secrets*, p. 286)

Another recommendation is to multiply the age by two and divide by ten, therefore: 30 years x 2 = 60 divided by 10 = 6 days between ejaculations. But with any of these formulas it is important to understand that they are only guidelines and that a wide range of important factors must be considered, including heredity, age, basic health, and stress levels. Intellectual and sensitivity levels and lifestyles also need to be taken into account. It might be a good idea to set a personal goal for the ideal number of ejaculations for every ten coitions, say three times out of ten. With increased practice, one can move gradually toward the goal, but never with a rigid attitude, nor with any pressure or guilt. On the contrary, these methods should bring into lovemaking a more conscious, joyful, and playlike quality.

Men, after only a few months of practicing spermatic control, report that the conscious discipline of the physical technique can drop back into the unconscious level of mind as the body, now conditioned by the extraordinary pleasure levels, will more or less automatically refrain from ejaculating. The pumping of the perineum in drawing the sperm inward reaches a feeling level similar to the spasm of ejaculation. As the woman becomes more and more reliant on the control of her partner, she is further released into a deeper level of abandonment and sensation.

The success of all these techniques is dependent upon the cooperation of the woman. *E.S.O.*, a popular sex manual by Alan and Donna Brauer, provides detailed instruction on how to extend sexual orgasm in both men and women. Brauer describes the role of women in assisting the male partner in gaining control over ejaculation:

> At first you and your partner will have to pay close attention to controlling ejaculation. When you bring him up to the high level of arousal near ejaculation, he'll feel close to going over. You have to be very careful then, watching his signs of arousal and stopping or lightening and changing stimulation when he gets too close. . . . Control becomes a matter of teamwork: you sense his level of arousal and change rhythm and stroke to help him with the control; at the same time, he responds with muscular contractions and relaxations and by bearing down. . . . It's important to remember that the man's ejaculation isn't the woman's goal. When your partner approaches ejaculation, the woman should reduce stimulation, not increase it. . . . If a man doesn't know about the much greater amount of pleasure in controlled and

extended intercourse, he pushes for ejaculation. The woman must be strong and help him resist this urge. If you give in too soon and stimulate him to ejaculation, you will be robbing him of a greater pleasure, and he may feel responsible for failing to control himself. (p.116-18)

Most other sources that outline the principles of semen retention and non-ejaculatory orgasms are based on ideas derived from Eastern philosophies and are cloaked in terminology from Indian and Chinese yogic practices. Much of this literature indicates three different approaches, which men may choose according to their own temperament and needs: the first is to prolong intercourse before allowing ejaculation; the second is to completely prevent ejaculation or only allow ejaculation infrequently (the Eastern approach); the third is, as found in E.S.O., to extend the duration of the orgasmic spasm itself.

If we unwrap these ideas we find, in all of them, a sound scientific basis. One of the more interesting is that the sex hormones which make up the spermatic fluid are the same hormones that contribute to the formation of the male sexual characteristics and traits during adolescence. According to this theory, when the male retains and reabsorbs his sexual fluids, these hormones are reabsorbed into his system and continue to maintain and intensify an individual's sexuality. This theory states that men who habitually lose their semen through sexuality (a moderate estimate is that the average Western male has five thousand orgasms in a lifetime) actually neutralize and deplete their sexual identity. This explains why male maturity and old age, in our society, is marked by an outward appearance of declining sexual appeal and energy.[8] Thus, when a man preserves his masculinity through semen retention his identity as a male is fortified. In Western society the tendency for some men, after a few years of marriage, to constantly seek the companionship of other men may result from a need to compensate for, and externally reinforce, their sense of masculinity, which has been diminished by semen loss through sex with women.

One obvious side benefit of semen retention is contraception. These techniques if used carefully can free sexuality from the shadow of unwanted pregnancy. Most women in the Western world have been programmed to fear sex because of the fear of unwanted pregnancy and, for this reason more than any other, sex has been associated with sin. Modern methods of contraception have disastrous side effects for women. For example, the

Pill has clinically been shown to have extensive and numerous detrimental side effects on women's health. More recently, at an international conference on AIDS it was reported that the Pill increased women's susceptibility to AIDS. New research from Africa suggests women on the Pill are two to three times more likely to become infected. A more subtle effect of the Pill is noted by sociologist, Lionel Tiger who states that when a woman takes the Pill, because of the hormones it contains, she walks around in a state which can only be called pseudo-pregnant. The Pill also blocks her from producing the hormones and pheromones that make her most sexually attractive to men. When the Pill is administered to female macaque monkeys, a species similar to humans in many ways, the response is nothing short of disturbing: the males simply stop breeding and are not interested in the females at all. The males then resort to sexual behavior patterns almost exclusively with other males.[9] Although no definitive parallel can be made, it is significant that the utilization of the Pill throughout the Western world is concurrent with an enormous rise in male homosexuality.

Worse than the Pill is the IUD scandal in which many women became terribly infected, or even sterile, and aborted. The suffering and injury that abortions cause women in the West are bad enough, but it is miniscule compared with statistics now emerging from modern Russia, with its massive, patriarchal state society. Western researchers estimate that there are three abortions for every live Soviet birth. Many women tell of having six, seven, or even eight abortions, and they may even be the lucky ones. Since anesthesia is not used in state-subsidized abortions, many seek out private arrangements. They may get the anesthesia, but the risk of complications is apparently greater than in a hospital. One third of all women who opt for private abortions die from the operation. Prospects for improvement on that front are remote. Abortion is the main means of contraception in the Soviet Union because of a lack of other contraceptive options. Russian women take a stoic attitude toward these humiliating conditions. One Russian housewife cited in *Time Magazine* commented, "If a man does not want to be careful, what can you do?"[10]

In a future society, men must take the responsibility for the destination of their seed. Women are burdened enough with the reproductive process and, in the new balance of sexuality, birth control should be predominantly based on male control of ejaculation. This training should take place routinely in adolescence, just as toilet training takes place in early childhood. The philosophy of sexual freedom and the release of sexuality from repression will make sense only when methods exist to definitely ensure that sexuality does not lead to the despair of unwanted pregnancy. Freedom from sexual repression must be accompanied by the assurance that sexuality leads to pleasure, not pain. Ejaculation control is the simplest, most direct means of gaining that assurance.

A Spiritual Sense of Sexuality

Apart from the practical value of ejaculation control, there are psychological and spiritual values, plus an increase in plain old pleasure. The will and self-control that a man exercises in order to retain his semen is the same will he exercises in his struggle with life. It is a will that seeks to transcend one of the most powerful of all biological states and, if he is successful in mastering his ejaculation, there lie beyond possibilities for sexual pleasure and ecstasy that are completely unknown and unexpected. There is an intensification of pleasure that makes every stroke in the act of intercourse equal to the pleasure that is associated with a normal emission. This form of internalized male sexual orgasm allows him to taste the quality and levels of female orgasm. In Jungian terminology, it is the mechanism by which he comes into contact with his own internal feminine power (the anima). In general, the real value is for a man to seek the transcendent. The power of transcendence is what a man really has to offer to the world and the women in his life. A man who does not transcend in some mode of life, be it in virtue or honor or skill or creativity or excellence of performance, contributes very little to life. Unlike women, who are able to contribute and create simply through their natural and biological being, a man must in some way seek the will toward and techniques of self-transcendence. This transcendence can now be approached with a powerful physiological base, such as mastery of ejaculation.

Besides the benefits for a man in retaining his own sexual identity, these techniques have an obvious positive effect on a man's relationship with a woman. Typically, the sexual attraction between a man and a woman declines with the duration of the relationship. Certainly, the practice of semen retention would sustain the heightened levels of desire that a man feels for a woman and could conceivably prevent this decline. Also, the techniques involved in semen retention lend greater variety and heightened pleasure to the sexual act. Longer relationships provide a greater possibility for cultivating these techniques, thereby giving a purposefulness to long term male/female relationships. The drain on a man's energies and the satiation of his desires due to too frequent ejaculation are obvious. Semen retention and absorption generate an elixir that would allow him to maintain his masculine prowess, increase his longevity, and diminish his subconscious, if not conscious, resentment toward the female in his life. The fear and antagonism toward women in several ancient cultures such as Greece, noted in the writing of philosophers such as Plato, may be traced to the fact that some women have either a procreative instinct or a psychological need to draw the semen out of men. This causes a loss to both a man's physical and spiritual energy. In modern times, the unbearable hostilities that so often develop in marriages or long term relationships can possibly be traced to this same source. There is possibly no better basis to present day male/female relationships than women helping their men aqcuire and master those techniques that can lead to the transformation of male sexuality appropriate to the newly emerging matriarchal age.

There is now an urgency for men and women to acquire new positive attitudes and sexual techniques. The anger, resentment, and misunderstanding between the sexes, due to long accumulated injustices has, within the last twenty years, begun to fester to a head. This mistrust between the sexes must be cleared before the phase of spiritual sexuality can begin. One key to the process of sexual restructuring is for feminist activists, as well as modern men, to understand that the subjection of females and female sexuality is not the result of male power, but rather male powerlessness. When the Christian church repressed and diminished female sexuality, male sexuality and power diminished with it. The drive for men to control and dominate women comes not out of a powerful inner sense of masculinity and masculine identity, but from an inner weakness and confusion. For women to feel that they can gain sexual equality by imitating the present male-dominated social roles such as business executives, lawyers, soldiers, priests, factory workers, etc., is an error. These role models, as they currently exist, are themselves exhibitions of weakened and distorted masculinity, the cover for male powerlessness.

The grounds for a society based on the spiritual sense of sexuality has several key components. The first and most important is the understanding that the main function of males in their relationships to females is to be devoted to the processes and science of giving women pleasure. These attitudes are particularly based on the giving of sexual pleasure, and the physical key to accomplishing this goal is for the male to cultivate his sexuality with an understanding that there is a difference between the *male sexual orgasm and ejaculation.*

A Taoist Interpretation

In Taoist thought from ancient China, men and women represent through their sexual attraction the primary polarity attraction that binds together the universe. In Taoist terminology it is the attraction of Yin and Yang; in Western physics it is the electromagnetic attraction between positive and negative polarities. In either case, according to the law of opposites, immediately after male ejaculation, the attraction between male and female is neutralized, and this neutralization of men and women contributes to the weakening of the dynamics of the entire universe. Again, we find Eastern philosophy tending to make direct connections between the things that we do in our ordinary life and larger universal themes. The theme of the "magical identity" between the individual consciousness and that of the collective, or universal, is becoming more and more prevalent in Western psychology. Here it is stated by J. Krishamurti from *The First and Last Freedom:*

> To transform the world we must begin with
> ourselves: and what is important in the beginning
> with ourselves is the intention . . . this is our
> responsibility, yours and mine; because, however
> small may be the world we live in, if we can bring
> about a radically different point of view in our daily
> existence then perhaps we shall affect the world at
> large.

The view that we change the world only by changing ourselves may be considered romantic and naive, but it is indisputable that a partial remedy to the present sexual crisis could be effected if both sexes were instructed at a very young age in this form of sexual control. It would: (1) bring a heightening of pleasure to both partners; (2) remove the fear of pregnancy without artificial methods of birth control; (3) stimulate male desire and tenderness toward the female; (4) build and regenerate physical health; and (5) contribute to spiritual growth, as well as to the enduring qualities of a relationship.

Stages of Development: Orgasmic Release or Retention

Another important consideration, very often ignored in the "Eastern" approach to orgasm, is the idea put forward by the pioneer psychiatrist, Wilhelm Reich. Reich assigned great importance to the full release of the orgasm in both men and women, believing that an unblocked surrender to the full ejaculative spasm was fundamental to psychological and physical health. This ability to release should grow concurrent with the full opening of the personality and was a key, in Reich's view, for the discovery of self and individuality.[11] The obvious wisdom of the Reichian view need not contradict a seemingly opposite process of ejaculation retention, if one assigns the first process to the early youthful stage of sexual experience and the latter to maturity. It seems to me that the sequential combination of Reich's view of orgasm and the Eastern view of orgasm may represent a picture of natural sexual evolution. First there is a growth into a powerful ejaculation, one which releases with it the voice, the pelvic rhythm, and the breath. Secondly, as the male matures, he finds that the ejaculation is intensified by maintaining and allowing for a build up before release. This stage is associated with an awareness of the increased pleasure being received by the woman as a result of his self-control. (The egoism of youthful sexual neediness gives way to a genuine ego-pride in being able to provoke enjoyment for his partner). The third stage then grows naturally into a more complete capacity for self-control, allowing for an injaculation of sperm and an intensification of sexuality, which is transcending for both the male and his partner. As it stands, with our present attitudes toward male sexuality, we have nowhere to grow with it; there is no conscious means of refining and extending the single most important means of human relationship. It is little wonder that a high percentage of men, out of ignorance and desperation, attempt to keep alive their sexual drive through promiscuity and infidelity. The familiarity of modern marriage deadens all the sensational and commercial stimulation that has been programmed into the male sexual response. This artificial stimulation vanishes under the sometimes bleak constraint of marriage and, at the same time, a man experiences a self-depletion caused by regular ejaculation. If clear techniques were available for deepening and cultivating sexual energy, both partners would realize that random, scattered affairs are uninteresting compared to the depth of intimacy possible through a sustained relationship. Now that AIDS has blocked the path of casual promiscuity, the evolution of a genuinely erotic tradition may be forthcoming in modern society.

11·

Patterns for a
New Ritual Sexuality

Once the patriarchal pattern of dominance/submission is broken in male/female sexual relationship, a magic, dramatic playfulness can open up for both sexual partners. She makes contact with her aggressiveness and, with that, the ability to initiate and seduce. She also gains access to all the dark, foreboding, perverse passions that are linked to love, tenderness, joy, and pleasure, through the natural connection of opposites inherent in universal femininity. Sexual play in the feminized mode is closely aligned to the theater. Remember that Dionysus, the god of feminine sexuality, is also the god of theater. It is unlike the male patriarchal sexual play derived from the sports arena. It is not a play based on the victor, nor is it concerned with the excitement generated by some final, irreversible notion of winning or losing. The male ritual of battling and struggling to win the desired object is really only appropriate to the preliminary courtship phase of sexuality. The patriarchal extension of the dominant/submissive, winning/losing mode to the sexual act itself causes great repression and diminution of sexual enjoyment and meaning.

In *Return of the Goddess*, Whitmont suggests that the feminine or human play is deliberate and microcosmic, as if a restaging of life's flowing dynamic:

In play, fantasy and practicality complement each other; mind measures itself, and experiments with existence. Play mobilizes and structures the powers of the unconscious psyche. It gives form to raw energy;

it civilizes. Through its symbolic, "as if" enactment play moves and transforms the player (and to a lesser degree) the involved spectator. Hence the cathartic effect of the symbolic enactment of the "life play" in the theatre, the original patron being no other than Dionysus himself. This god appeared, variously, as playing child to be cared for; raving mad power; Lord of Life and Death; an empty mask, appearing and disappearing. (*Return of the Goddess*, p.241)

There are many ritual methods, some of which we can use today to reinstate feminine-orientated sexuality, that is, a sexual enactment of feeling, impulse, fantasy that has become charged through passion with the energy and vision of the archetypes. The method that I have selected to relate is found in two seemingly unrelated sources. One source is that of the ancient eastern Tantric and Taoist traditions. The other is the Stanislavsky method-acting technique, which again reveals the fundamental connection between sexuality and dramatization. In method acting, the ritual is called the mirror exercise. The two partners stand face-to-face confronting each other and one partner simply mirrors every movement made by the other. In the sexual ritual, as in theater before the play begins, the background or setting is consciously considered. Those things that harmonize the mood of maleness with femaleness are the same today as they were in most ancient times: red or brilliantly colored flowers, sensual music, dancing and singing together, spontaneous laughter, pleasant or erotic odors, pure wine, or other inhibition-lowering intoxicants such as marijuana.

All of these set the stage for the kind of intense sexual excitement that can trigger psychological role-play. The mirror exercise is a simple yet excellent initiation into ritual sexuality: one partner moves and/or makes a sound, a gesture, an expression, or an emotional act, while the other partner as quickly and exactly as possible imitates that act. That is the first game rule. An optional game rule is for the second partner to just as quickly interpret the action and come back with its complementary response, i.e., the act of menacing is responded to with the act of being afraid. This mirroring ritual, according to Stanislavsky teachers, is the origin of all folk dance both recent and ancient, except perhaps modern isolated and alienated "do your own thing" disco dancing. The conscious one-pointed effort to mirror another person first brings about a breakdown in self-consciousness; each partner learns that he or she can play out and divulge many roles and attitudes that were hitherto kept hidden, even from themselves. This newly found intimacy brings about an unspoken communication and harmonization that, in time and through practice, dissolves into a complete, spontaneous flow between the partners. Mirroring is only one of many ritual forms. Another more commonly known form is enactment between partners of roles such as, master and slave, prostitute and patron. All these can, if performed with care so that no harm befalls the participants, provide excitement and psychological release.

Costumes may be added, but the positions that the body takes, as well as the various parts of the body involved in the act, are all the couple need to express the complete range of emotions, feelings, characteristics, and fantasies that are hiding inside all of us. The emerging feminized psychological view, which is toward completeness, in contrast with the patriarchal drive toward perfection, believes that every part contains the whole. The entire range of emotions and stereotypes is within each one of us. Within each one of us there is the ugly villain and the virtuous hero, the prostitute and the saint, the destructive exploiter and the pathetic victim, the wise and powerful father and the cowering child, the affectionate nurturing mother and the hungering needful waif. We are all stars and celebrities as well as retiring hermits, we are all both the sadist and the masochist, the philanderer and infidel, as well as the true and loyal lover. All these archetypal roles await expression through the free, passionate exchange of ritual sexuality. They can be more easily be assimilated into our personality and way of being through ritual than through an ethical process, or a disciplined acceptance of differences.

Although it varies with individual couples, very often, at first, it is the women who will lead the mirroring. This is especially advantageous around and during the time of menstruation. It is during menstruation that she descends into the dark world of unexplained, unprovoked feelings, those that are associated with disruption, despair, and death. In other words, she reflects the chaos of destructive elimination necessary for the process of new birth and regeneration. Through ritual the male is able to reflect back these feelings and make them more explainable and useful, instead of just avoiding and suffering the monthly feminine moodiness. The destructive-mood syndrome of the menstrual cycle is an important lever in the constant rhythm of change that every growing individual and relationship must ride and/or endure. The ritual allows men to surrender the patriarchal fear of change and the unknown, and to enter creatively into the nameless realm of feminine feeling.

Fortunately, there are now many books that give a great variety of sexual ritual forms. One of the best is Douglas and Slinger's *Sexual Secrets*. In this work and others there are a multitude of sexual positions, both coital and pre-coital, that evoke animal forms: the elephant, lion, monkey, snake, bird.[12] Just as specific animals arouse in us distinct emotional responses (i.e. the lion, courage and aggression), so these positions have the potential of moving us out of our single, locked-in self-definition, to a whole range of unexplored emotional depths. *As already stated, the male, in order to enter the magical theater of emotional release and exploration, must first acquire the technique of spermatic retention. He must shift the control and force that he used in the patriarchal age to repress his emotions and his feelings and applies it to a control over a bodily function.* So in principal, the relationship between aggression and sexuality is not broken, it is only moved to a different plane of being. This relationship, as has been stated, is a philosophical and biological truth of our being. In myth, the closeness of sexuality and aggression is expressed through the similarity in names of Eros, god of love and Ares, god of war. We can find the same similarity in our modern language in the relationship between the French word for love, "amour" and the English word "armor". This similarity is also reflected in the Indian myth where Shiva, the great god of sexuality and spiritual transformation, wears an armor that allows him to make love and behold the Goddess within the woman he desires without her enchantment robbing him of his seed. With this armor the Goddess can reveal to Shiva all her aspects, both the beautiful and the repellent and, in so doing, teach him the laws and mysteries of creation.[13]

Besides sexual positions and the mirroring activity, bodily parts also hold a key to the particular emotions that can be released through sexual ritual. Wilhelm Reich gave Western psychology a powerful tool for understanding ourselves, which is consistent with ancient philosophy. He said the physical body is the subconscious mind. Reich meant emphatically that the physical body and the subconscious mind are one and the same thing.[14] *The subconscious does not reside totally in a real or imagined portion of the brain but is in every way reflected in the parts, the forms, the proportions and postural alignments of the body.* In the same way, eroticism does not reside in one portion of the body; the enitre body has an erotic role to play in ritual sexuality: mouth, ears, anus, feet, elbows, etc., all have erotic potential. Each part is a reservoir of particular emotions and its stimulation can trigger the release of these emotions. The more obvious of these associations are, for example, the center of the chest with our more tender needs for affection and self-protection; the thighs and their association with our will, assertion, and drive; the neck and shoulders with our ego and sense of pride; the anus with our shadowy, depersonalized sense of rejection, etc. We carry ourselves, we move, we breathe, in patterns that are dictated by the emotional injuries and the neurological and muscular excesses or deficiencies in these distinct regions of our bodies.

As a man and woman come to truly know themselves and each other, the shadowy or violent projections withheld in these regions can be released and explored within the deepest pleasures of ritual sexuality. This form of total bodily acceptance and involvement encourages a concern for one's health and hygiene, so that one's entire body becomes an instrument in the service of love and pleasure. Exercise, combined with the right kinds of food, positively affects the erotic smell, texture, and vibration of the body. Hygienic practices regarding the colon are important in this regard. A polluted, obstructed colon prevents the muscular contractions needed for redirecting sexual energy and fluids. A clean, healthy body, with all the orifices and projections erotically available and involved, makes all the homosexual, bisexual, and heterosexual ritual variations available to each partner.

Another important advantage for a man that results from his seminal control is that he will be inclined to stabilize his breathing patterns, his diet, and his lifestyle. These advances will not be prompted by a disciplinarian attitude but will emerge out of the desire to increase and expand his erotic pleasures. Self-discipline that is motivated by a sense of increasing pleasure and desire in one's life is much different than that motivated by a sense of duty and forced control. It is the difference between a child running and playing freely in the wind and an office worker laboriously jogging in city traffic—the only similarity being that they are both running.

With semen conservation, a man will no longer be the victim of involuntary ejaculation and the meaningless loss of vital lifeforce that is associated with it. He will no longer stand before femininity with a sense of his own powerlessness and, due to that powerlessness, a need to control her. Instead, with a sense of inner power that can extend to every other level of life, he will be able to realize the highest goal of manhood—that of conscious giving. The beautiful paradox is that, when a man can prevent the surrender of his seed in orgasm, the intensification of passion enables him to surrender himself in total. This is precisely the nature of the sovereignty that women must now hold over men, and it is that which the feminine requests in the myth of Parsifal. With that sovereignty the order of the universe can begin to be restored.

I believe every male, whatever his type or season of life, whether he be heterosexual, homosexual or bisexual, lives through, and for, the love of the feminine. That woman, or feminine principle, can be within another male, within himself, or an external female. A man furthers his own life and destiny when he furthers the life and destiny of the women, or woman, he loves. This can be done by no better means than by being always erect and attracted, like an adolescent god, to the feminine principle in whatever way it manifests in the context of his life.

12·

Another Threefold View of Sexuality

In Chapter 3, we discussed the triadic phases of life and types of people defined by pre-sexual, sexual and post-sexual states of being. Here again we are suggesting a threefold view to connect stages of our sexuality to the three philosophical pursuits of life: Goodness, Beauty, and Truth. The first state of sexuality is called romantic love, which believes, in all its youthful explosiveness and magnetism, that it can find the completeness of itself in the object of its attractions and desires. In this stage of sexuality, it is not orgasmic control but the full release of the spasm that is the goal. It is in the romantic stage of love that care must be taken to avoid unwanted pregnancy. For this reason, a great many restrictions are placed on the meeting of the young lovers (astrologers are to be consulted, curfews, etc). The philosophers of romantic love also say that if the passion is high enough between the lovers, the heat will destroy the fertility potential of the sperm. Romantic love is involved with the ethical pursuit of goodness.[15] There are always strong ethical undercurrents to romantic passions: loyalty, fidelity, virtue, honor and an often anguished idealization of the one and only. Through romantic love we develop our feeling nature, in the sense that it is by feeling that we confer value on ourselves and on the world around us. The object of our romantic love *becomes the ultimate value for us*, and all our values are colored by the intensity of that romantic passion. In the Middle Ages, romantic love reigned to the point of obsession. The beautiful, sexually unapproachable woman became to the man an image of the goodness of his own soul. This extreme idealization unfortunately contributed to, as we have said, its polar opposite in the centuries of witchhunts that followed. In the minds of European males following the Middle Ages, idealized femininity transformed into its own opposite, the dark and vile witch (from the complete good to the complete evil).

As love matures, the second stage is the ritualization of sexuality, where both partners, through their relationship, expand and release the emotional energies upon which the manifestation of their full individuality depends. The modern search for physical health and bodily perfection is incomplete and impossible without first obtaining emotional and psychological health. Ritual sexuality controls and aids this process. This second stage in the evolution of sexuality, ritual lovemaking, is absorbed with the aesthetic pursuit of beauty. In ancient times, the source of all art and beauty was mythology and the enactment of myth through ritual. Through Jungian psychology, mythical characters are shown to be personifications of our own inner moods. Moods are unprovoked, universal states of being, such as gloom, anger, possession, joy, and cruelty. These primary internal conditions drive human action in all epochs and cultures: they are the pure dramatic forces of life that descend upon us from the unknown archetypal world[16]—a world in which individuals can participate through an understanding of ritual sexuality.

The third stage of sexuality, which I call regenerative, is described very frequently in ancient Chinese texts. This we might say is the stage of sexuality that is centered upon physical health and longevity, transcendental awareness, and a deep knowledge of the body and its energies. For this stage, spermatic retention becomes even more exacting, but it is more easily accomplished because of the maturity of the man and perhaps the relationship. This stage requires some understanding of reflexology and acupuncture. Acupuncture meridians are pathways transversing the entire surface of the body, carrying energies that maintain the organs and organ functions of the body. There are postures and positions and breathing techniques related to sexuality that, through activating particular acupuncture meridians, can help to prevent or overcome dysfunctioning, for example, in the liver or kidneys or heart. There are several texts that are excellent guides for developing this phase of sexuality, such as *Taoist Secrets of Love and Healing Love Through the Tao, and The Tao of Sexology: The Book of Infinite Wisdom* and *The Complete System of Self Healing*, both by Dr. S. T. Chang.[17]

The regenerative stage of sexuality is focused upon knowledge in the sense of the ancient Greek word Logos. The Greek notion of Logos is derived from the same source as our concept of analogy. Analogy is the comprehensive process of conferring meaning through relating one aspect of experience to another. The mathematical formula for the analogical process is the same as that of the geometric proportion and progression: A is to B as B is to C (A/B as B/C). Since living nature multiplies, grows, and creates forms through the same geometric, proportional, and progressional systems, the ancient Greeks concluded that the laws and forces that govern the creation of things are the same laws and forces that allow for their comprehension. In their philosophy, the Logos became the controlling and binding principle of the Universe. It is this binding principle of the Logos that draws into relationship the positively, negatively, and neutrally charged particles of the atom. The same cohesive principle maintains the bonds in molecular structures and in interrelationship of all parts with wholes. On the level of mind, Logos is the principle that draws together the diverse phenomenom of our perception, through association and metaphor, to maintain the structures of intellect. A Hindu Upanishad (Taittiraya) refers to this principle: "I am the link between, I am the link between, I am the sustaining principle of the Universe. He who knows me knows divine knowledge."

In Greek philosophy the principle of analogical wisdom was always revealed to man by a goddess. The feminine, expansive analogical mode of thought is in stark contrast to the male systematic and reductionist logic, which attempts to establish abstract equational identities. Human thought and activity that adheres to the form and pattern of the Logos principle was considered to actually participate in the creative mind of Mother Nature. The human body was considered the link or Logos between the Universal polarity of the Earth and Sky. The knowledge of how the celestial and terrestrial rhythms and movements harmonized and interacted in the human body is the "Logos" upon which regenerative sexuality is based.

Ancient philosophies acknowledge an all-pervading life force, which animated physical, intellectual, and psychological phenomena (prana). Modern scientific philosophy has denied the existence of such a force but our word emotion, as it's etymology—"that which causes movement"—suggests, correlates to the idea of the Universal emotive force. Emotion, thus defined, is that pure, universal, highly charged life energy underlying all other physical and psychological movements, whether they be changes in bodily conditions, moods, feelings, or thoughts.

The goal of regenerative sexuality is to understand the ebb

and flow of the Universal emotive force as it moves from planetary, solar and lunar levels and through the principle of Logos connects to the corresponding energy qualities in plants, animals, and minerals and the organs and nerves of our bodies. Through regenerative sex we can learn to constructively balance and direct these forces for the maintenance and pleasure of our bodies. More importantly, these sexual disciplines become great teachers for understanding the laws of nature. This mature stage of sexuality becomes much less personal and can include variations of sometimes three or more participants.[18]

We can trace, then, three major stages of sexual expression: the romantic stage, the ritual stage, and the regenerative or therapeutic stage. Each of these stages is connected to one of the three primary philosophical pursuits of life, which Plato claimed gives life all its meaning: the pursuit of *Goodness*, *Beauty*, and *Truth*. These interrelationships are shown in Diagram 5. As Schwallar de Lubicz wrote in *The Temple of Man*: "It is impossible for us to learn elsewhere what we are incapable of learning within our own bodies."

The Powers of Regenerative Sex

The concepts of regenerative sex are very far removed from our ordinary sexual attitudes. Recent exposure to Eastern healing arts, such as Chinese acupuncture, and innovative massage practices, such as reflexology, are providing access to this important function of our sexuality. In both these healing systems certain sensitized body regions (in acupuncture, the ear; in reflexology, the feet, hands, and genitals) act as a microcosm for the entire

DIAGRAM 5. SEXUAL DEVELOPMENT AND PHILOSOPHY

Each of the three stages of sexuality can be considered as counterpart of the three goals of philosophy: the pursuit of the Good, the Beautiful, and the True.

Philosophical Pursuit	Greek Description	Primary Concern	Stage of Sexuality
Goodness	Ethos (Ethics)	Feelings	Romantic Love
Beauty	Mythos (Myth)	Moods	Ritual Sexuality
Truth	Logos (Logic)	Emotions	Regenerative Sexuality

body. Chinese acupuncture views the body as a network of meridian lines (near the body's surface) that extend from head to
toe. These meridians or channels carry energy, interconnecting
and harmonizing the activities of the major bodily organs. Reflexology is similar except it is more concerned with the flow
of neural energy and with regions or zones of nerve endings near
the surface of the body that (like acupuncture meridians), connect to all the major organs. The genitals in both sexes are special reflexology zones through which all other parts of the body,
internal and external, can be effected. Pressure can be applied
to specific points on the gland at the head of the penis, as well
as other specific points along the shaft extending to the scrotum
and the anus; this massage will stimulate and energize the functions of the heart (on the very tip), lungs, liver, spleen, kidneys,
prostate, etc. Using this knowledge, sex can be performed with
religious regularity, like "morning and evening prayer" and, as
prayer should do, it can balance, center, and harmonize the energy in both partners. Masturbation (as long as ejaculation is
avoided) can have positive and necessary health benefits during
periods without a sexual partner. Attitudes about sex in Eastern
texts generally emphasize the understanding its relationship to
beauty, health, hygiene, and the considerable psychospiritual
power it can generate.

Of further interest is the theory described by Dr. S. T. Chang
in The Tao of Sexology; this theory concerns the location of the
heart point on the male and female genitals.[19] The point that
stimulates the heart flow of energy in the male is on the very
tip of the penis, while it is the very deepest point inside the
female vagina, beyond finger reach. Only through very deep penetration do the heart points of the male and female stimulate
each other. It is only the male penis that can stimulate the heart
point of a woman; artificial sexual aids are not effective because
this level of stimulation requires the energies surrounding living
tissue.[20] The seemingly unbalanced dependency of women on
the male sex organ for their sexual fulfillment is actually small
compared to the complete dependency that men have on the
life-giving, life-sustaining power of women and on the feminine
principle of Earth. Modern Darwinian sex theorists, such as
Richard Dawkins (The Selfish Gene) and John Gribbins (The Re-
dundant Male) claim, in the light of laboratory techniques such
as cloning, artificial insemination, and genetic engineering, that
the male is sexually and reproductively obsolete. Dr. Chang's
discussion of energy points found on the genitals affirms that
men are neither sexually nor reproductively expendable. The

stimulation of the heart center is essential to the longevity and the maturation of the "feeling", intuitive quality of feminine intelligence. This intelligence is of critical importance in the transition now facing humanity.

According to Dr. Chang's theory, by understanding the reflexology points on his penis a man can, through non-ejaculatory masturbation, stimulate and maintain his entire psychophysical energy level; this may account for the isolated roles and lifestyles of men, such as solitary soldiers, sailors, wanderers, saints, priests, hermits, etc. Women, on the contrary, cannot completely balance or stimulate themselves without sexual contact with a man. Perhaps men will not become obsolete if and when they understand that their role in relationship to woman is, through the heart reflex point, to provide balance, pleasure, excitement, and insight to the feminine principal in its sacrificial labor of creating, generating, and nourishing the living universe.

This ancient sexual philosophy, from Taoist and Tantric texts, has not been polluted by the puritanical antierotic doctrines of the patriarchal monotheistic religions such as Buddhism, Christianity, Judaism, or Islam. Dr. Chang in *The Tao of Sexology* notes:

> From the Taoist viewpoint, practicing celibacy is about the most harmful thing you can do to your body. Denying attention or the right to function to any part of your body is foolish, as foolish as rejecting the use of your eyes and ears. Not using any portion of your body for its normal purpose will create a harmful imbalance which can affect every other part of your body, since all bodily functions are interconnected. Those religions that encourage celibacy do so out of the realization that excessive sex can deplete the pineal gland and then block communication with God. What is overlooked by these religions is the fact that celibacy can cause atrophy of the sexual and pineal glands. Cancer of the prostate in the male and cancer or atrophy of the uterus and ovaries in the female cannot be proper religious goals. (p.191)

Another important aspect of regenerative sexuality is also associated with the theory of acupuncture. According to this theory, our mental energies and abilities reside not in our brains, which only arrange and store information, but in the organs of the body. For example, the liver, and the energy flow associated with it, are the basis for the initial phase of mental activity: the inspirational conceptual moment of fresh insight. This mental activity is like the first envisioning of, for example, a beautiful building. If the liver function is below par, then this type of mental activity will also be impaired. The second phase of thought processes is the devising of a general structure or abstract plan to stabilize or materialize our vision. In the case of a building, this would be the architectural design. This secondary mental phase, which takes in all the aspects of an initial idea and then converts it into a logical structural model or plan of action, is dependent on the spleen and pancreas and associated meridian. If these organs are impaired, then the power of logical thought is affected.[21] This is the same for all the major classifications of mental processes: each has a bodily organ that generates and sustains its required level of energy. The kidneys govern the will power aspect of thought. A person with weak kidneys will tend to be fearful and lack the will power for clear, unclouded decisions. The lungs control the feeling content in thought and weak lungs cause overly emotional or sentimental thinking.

Sexual experience is the deepest, most powerful and complete bodily stimulation. By cutting off the full development of sexual stimulation, we, in affect, cut off the most organic and natural form of stimulation of our mental processes. Patriarchal society seems to produce leaders of government and industry who consistently guide humanity toward policies that are self-destructive and destructive toward the life of our planet. We can no longer ignore the fact that the harmonization of certain bodily energies controls the evolution of our intellectual capacities, and that this harmonization is dependent in part upon the deep powers contained in our sexual energies and a more conscious understanding of sexual stimulation.

Sex and the Seasons of Life

Each of the three stages of sexuality corresponds to different stages of one's lifetime, or to a particular quality or goal that may prevail throughout an entire lifetime. Like the seasons of a year, each phase has a different intention, quality of energy, technique, and value. No one phase is higher or preferable to another. We need simply to discover the potential of each of these patterns and find how it applies to our own life and development.

From birth to twenty-one years of age constitutes springtime, with the crisis of adolescence near the midpoint of the season: eleven or twelve years of age is the dawn of puberty or adolescence. At this midpoint, sexuality is oriented toward romantic love. This emphasis on romantic love generally continues until the early thirties (the thirties crisis), which is the midpoint of the summertime of life (twenty one years to forty two years). Generally, in the early thirties, we witness the passing of the last values and goals derived from childhood, family, conventional religion, and society. With this, the propensity toward romantic-dominated sexuality very often passes and is replaced with the freedoms and explorations of ritual sexuality but, as in nature, the qualities of the previous season often linger or reappear periodically through the new phase. Unfortunately, as our society only teaches, condones, and cultivates a commercialized version of romantic love, this new phase is very often characterized by disillusionment, hurt, and desperate affairs that follow the shattering of the romantic dream. In the ancient philosophy of sex and the seasons of life, this dead end is avoided.

The autumn phase is from forty-two to sixty-three years of life, with the midpoint of this season being the midlife crisis occurring from the early to mid-fifties. Again, at the midpoint age, ritual-based sexuality should give way to the regenerative form, which can be sustained, through the discipline of spermatic retention, as long into the winter of life (sixty-three to

DIAGRAM 6. SEXUALITY AND THE SEASONS OF LIFE

Spring		Summer		Autumn		Winter	
0 11–13	21	30–33	42	50–54	63	70–75	84
Feminine Dominant	Masculine Dominant		Feminine Dominant		Masculine Dominant		
Romantic			Ritual		Regenerative		

eighty-four years of life) as one desires. This is, of course, only a general outline, not a recipe to be applied rigidly. But it holds with it a hope that sexuality, with all its intensity and tenderness, need not evaporate with youth, leaving the remainder of life cold and physically unimpassioned.

The oscillation between male-dominant sexuality and society and female-dominant sexuality and society, which causes the growth and change in human history, is also mirrored in the evolution of our individual sexuality. The first half of the romantic stage of life, up to puberty, is completely dominated by the feminine; both male and female emerge from the womb and the maternal is the dominating force on every level of life. During the second half of the romantic love stage, which continues into the early thirties, this domination switches from the feminine to the masculine. In romantic love the man is the pursuer, the lover, the conqueror. Romantic love should develop the male qualities of courage, competitiveness, will, self-assertion, and achievement of a desired goal. With the emergence of the second phase of sexuality, ritual love, femininity again becomes the driving force. In ritual love, the woman learns the art of the Enchantress and the Initiatrix. Through ecstatic states, she leads her man in discovering the archetypal forces that control and release emotional states, as well as the forces that control the formation of matter itself. The third stage of sexuality switches again to male dominance. Regenerative sexuality is based on the idea that the human body is a microcosm of the ebb and flow of universal energies. Here we find a very male-oriented body of knowledge that guides sexuality, and its effect on health and longevity, in the latter years of life. This knowledge contains information as to how the different physical organs are affected by time of day, different body positions, and the varied thrusting rhythms and patterns used in sexual intercourse. After the third phase of life is concluded, the final stage of life, which is death, is again female dominated. It is the merging back into the universal ground, out of which our moment of individuality arose.

The division of sexual life into the natural seasons is paralleled by the division of men into one of three general categories. In the first are men who are predominantly intellectual and/or spiritually inclined, such as philosophers, poets, scientists, academics, clergy, clerics, and engineers. In the second are men who are characterized by their vitality, that is, artists, performers, designers, businessmen, and all those who are involved with expressive and/or aesthetic work. In the third are men who are physical and inclined to manual labor, including builders, farmers, mechanics, etc. Each of these three predominantly different types of men will have a particular way of relating to the three phases of sexuality outlined above, as well as to the seasonal changes of life. Therefore this outline of the general divisions of the evolution of male sexual energy, its seasons, and its types is meant to provide a sort of lasting universal structure within which one can explore the profound powers of sexuality. It is not meant to establish some new standard of normality, but instead should be applied to life as a guide that relates our intensely personal experience to the whole of universal energies and cyclical changes.

13·

Social Organization and Sexuality: Past and Future

Approximately five thousand years ago, our European sexual attitudes and institutions began to grow out of a strange hybridization: an invading patriarchal nomadic horde, conquering and merging into very ancient declining, matriarchal, sedentary societies. In this hybridization, many of the social traditions of each became intermixed. The conquering Aryan patriarchy set up their male-dominant domestic and legislative forms (lording) over the old matriarchies, while at the same time being "civilized" by them.

Matriarchal Societies

In the older matriarchies the management and administrative functions in society were handled by women. The social order was an extension of the household and feminine characteristics were therefore much better suited to these roles. Feminine characteristics, such as the procreating, nourishing, and protecting instincts, were sources for the sort of drives toward pluralism and continuity that are necessary for the material foundation of life. This base then allowed for the horizontal expansion of the family group and collective. Femininity, linked to the fertility cycles of nature through ritual, generates the conventions, traditions, and habits necessary to form the living social norms upon which society is based. In Greek mythology, Athena, the female goddess of cities, symbolizes this type of feminine organization, which is conducive to urban collective order. This myth depicts the arrival of the nomadic invaders, when Athena becomes dominated by Zeus, the male patriarchal God. When this occurs, collective organization takes on the male propensity toward perfectionism, centralization, and abstract ideal standards of law and order, along with a single puritanical religion and morality. In other words, patriarchal organizations tend to serve their own abstract logic and consistency, rather than protect and nourish the raison d'être for society: human life in all its diversity. In the matriarchal society, the fundamental management of the social order was always in the hands of the women. In today's male-dominant corporate world, the feminine superiority for management is exploited and very often unacknowledged. The stereotype of the big business executive, who is really only a figurehead, while his female secretary holds the keys to power through her natural grasp of organizational information and timing, is an effective metaphor for the history of matriarchies being presided over by their patriarchal conquerors—the boss!

In *Les Quatre Sens de la Vie*, Alain Danielou describes ancient Indian society and marital customs believed to have been in existence prior to the Aryan invasions of India over four thousand years ago. Danielou's research shows that the extraordinarily refined Dravidian city states of Harappa and Mohenjodaro in the Indus valley provides a valuable model for social organization. First of all, women married at around thirteen or fourteen years of age. These were arranged marriages to which they were not bound for life but only for the phase in life centered on childbirth. (This conformed to nature in the sense that girls in early adolescence have very strong sexual urges, which contemporary society forces them to repress; this repression very often results in a fanatic hero worship of pop stars, etc.)

Usually, children in ancient Indian society remained in the family home only until they were about eight years old and then went on to live and receive an education from teachers who would ensure their language and numerate skills and then on to a teacher who would train them in their vocational craft. In other words, the mother was only the first teacher of a child and, even if she had several children, she could be free of her maternal responsibilities by the time she was in her late twenties or early thirties. The same pattern is found in tribal societies, such as the Australian Aborigines, where the male child parts contact with his mother in early adolescence and then, while living only with male tribal members, goes through a series of initiations, leading to manhood.

By their late twenties, early thirties, women typically begin to be interested in abstract philosophical or scientific studies or involvements. Since the marriage dissolved after the children had left the home, a woman was then free to pursue her intellectual or aesthetic development. This meant that she could fulfill her maternal and instinctual nature, as well as pursue an individual and intellectual development, without facing the dreadful double bind that modern women face in having to choose between career or marriage, or the difficult ordeal of being a working mother.

During their adolescent years, young people in this tradition had access to sexuality through a marriage that is supportive and reinforced by the extended family and the village system. This contrasts with the repression and hardship of adolescence; in modern society, this time is the most confusing, traumatic, and self-destructive of all the phases of human development.

In ancient Indian society, if the marriage dissolved after childrearing was completed, the woman might pursue an adult sex life, which could include a number of different partners, without there being any social stigma. If she were a highly erotic woman, she might become involved in the refined science of pleasure afforded by the temple, which maintained a tradition of sexual initiation related to spiritual development.

There was thus an attempt by these ancient societies to maintain a harmony with biological nature. Boys entered the marriage not quite as young, usually sixteen to twenty years of age. This precluded the phase of adolescence that, in our culture, is marked by violent sexual repression and self-destruction. It is during this period that a vital young male, with limited access to sexuality, turns to the use of alcohol and tobacco plus homosexuality, all of which dull and diminish the pressures of repressions. In ancient Indian cultures, males were only held to being providers during their period of raising children. They were released from their household responsibilities at an appropriate age to pursue their interests in sports, philosophy, or their own spiritual realization. Here was a social and marital institution that was more in rhythm with the natural evolution of the human body. Human beings were not forced to fit their biological rhythms around being efficient cogs in a vast industrial social machine.[22]

This description of a marital institution in an ancient society is *not* meant to be taken as a recipe for the modern world. However, it does show that we can make our sexual, social, and industrial institutions more applicable to our biological and psychological nature.

In the future, society must be organized in ways appropriate to the human psyche. Our psyche is based on the dynamics of sexuality and the balancing of our external sexuality with our internal. Open competition for roles through the battle of the sexes, or through individuals or groups endlessly pitted against one another, has had grave consequences. Instead, there should be in the future more of a harmonization of strengths and weaknesses, and the privileges and responsibilities, inherent in the sexes and in various types of individuals. If a male-dominant society becomes overidentified with its male aggressive dynamic, it will become impotent, just as an individual male who overidentifies with the aggressive, macho male image becomes trapped in the impotent form of sublimated homosexuality, resulting from excessive maleness.[23] We can build armies and sporting teams on this type of excessive male bonding pattern, but not a complete society. Likewise, a female-dominant society that overidentifies with its recessive female state becomes frigid. Both impotency and frigidity lead to a cessation of creativity and life in individuals and in societies.

Ancient societies provide us with interesting examples of how the anima/animus of a living society were balanced. In ancient Indian society, balance was achieved through male-female variations in different castes. For example, the peasant class was made up of farmers, artisans, and workers. This caste, which dealt primarily with the material aspects of life, was, in the external forms and institutions, dominated by women. Titles, wealth, and property were passed through the woman. Men were subsidiary to female power in all areas of family, business, and village organization, but they had more power and authority in the internal aspects of life, spirituality, religion, and ritual. The men worked in the fields, wandered, hunted, played games, studied traditions, investigated the occult and supernatural, and pontificated over theater and ritual. In this caste, internal life was dominated by the worship of male phallic energy, as demonstrated by its engagement in wild, phallic, fertility ceremonies. Female energy prevailed in the external life of this society. This caste was polygamist, polytheistic (worshiped many Gods) and promiscuous. It was vital, physical, and sensually and sexually active.

Within the same society, the priest or academic caste (known as the Brahmins), those who worked predominantly with their intellects and introspective faculties of meditation, had exactly the opposite balance of internal/external, male/female energies. In this caste male ethics, with rigid ideals and disciplines, governed external life. Food, clothing, sexuality, marriage, and all the external social institutions bore the mark of the highest standardized patriarchal codes of law and ethics. While the Brahmins' external lives were dominated by male energies and institutions, in their internal or spiritual life they worshiped the Divine Mother and the feminine principal as the highest deity. Women, while virtually absent from external life, were held in great spiritual reverence and respect.[24]

One may say that this social ideal, because it came from a caste society, is no longer relevant to us, but is this really the case? Our egalitarian society still maintains the outline of the caste system. Today we call it the working class, the middle class, the upper class, etc. Sadly, in modern society these divisions are supposedly determined only by the amount of money that people accumulate. In past societies, social division was determined by the different qualities and attributes among people. In a limited sense, this is true today. The worker, the artisan, the laborer, the builder, and the farmer, each has his own particular genius and quality and should have rights and responsibilities in society that are particular to his needs and strengths. These may include differences in sexual, marital, and moral codes, differences in clothing and dietary requirements, differences in religious and spiritual forms, differences in bonding and aggression patterns. This is equally true of the other natural divisions in societies. For example, the academic and professional class has also its own genius and its own needs, different from those of the working class, or indeed the business or commercial class or, for that matter, the military. Unfortunately, all these human variations in modern society must bend to standardized institutions, legal and social codes, which are most appropriately suitable to the business and commercial class. This of course is one of the most disturbing aspects of modern society. The business and commercial class dominates all other domains of life under capitalist democracies and, covertly, in the various forms of socialism. This domination of the business class goes back to the conquering patriarchal nomads who became predominantly mercantile traders, with a "shepherd's mentality" for controlling the herd. Neither socialism nor capitalism reflects the full nature and order of human society; all social institutions are totally economically and materialistically oriented.

The pressure in democratic and socialistic societies to level and equalize human population groups may, in some aspects, constitute an "enlightened" and modern political system, but it may be completely inappropriate when applied to human sexuality. Egalitarianism, that is, everything being equal for everybody, sounds fine as an abstract ideal, but men and women are different. The vast natural differences between the sexes are what make life intriguing and beautiful: the harmonization and amplification of difference between men and women, a composition of varied responsibilities and privileges at different levels of society, may make for a healthier dynamic and model for sexuality in future societies.

The patriarchal mindset forgets that the egalitarian ideal is connected, like light is to dark, to its opposite, totalitarianism. Behind the scenes of many socialistic and egalitarian societies, hidden oligarchies form—power groups that covertly manipulate and direct society. The matriarchal form of social organization is a functional hierarchy that itself is a linking of opposites, just as the apex of a triangle is connected to its base. Hierarchy, in all living systems, is not based on power or subjugation but differentiation of function. Brain cells, for example, function differently from liver cells and require a different oxygen intake, blood, and nutrient requirements and possess different metabolic and regenerative regulations, etc. The quality of a natural, functional hierarchy was the basis of social order in most developed ancient societies. Similar functional differences determined the social norms, for example, between the priest caste (brain cells) and the artisan (liver cells). We can turn to nature to find models for restructuring our present egalitarian facade, which covers a class division based on wealth and power.

All living organisms depend upon a hierarchical organization. Since human society can be considered to be the largest living organism on earth, it is important to utilize the natural principle as a model for social organization. The moment of death can thus be defined as the breakdown of hierarchical organization and complete leveling in the living system.

I am proposing that living nature serve as our model for the formation of our psychology and our society. Edward Whitmont, in *Return of The Goddess*, gives a description of the process of fertilization of the female egg by the male sperm; it provides an excellent model for the inversing and balancing of male/female energy that we have just described in ancient Indian social orders. He says:

> The feminine sex system, and the behavior of the egg
> cell especially, on first sight convey an image of
> passive, receptive, and engulfing behavior. There is a
> quiescent openness, ready to receive. In dramatic
> contrast to this static, quiescent immobility are the

thousands of restlessly swarming spermatozoa, aggressively seeking to penetrate. However, this is only an external view. As soon as the action shifts inward, masculine is no longer aggressively active, but, having spent its energy, becomes passive; the feminine, from its inner depths, now moves forth and takes charge. The sperm cell is dissolved, annihilated by the enzymes within the ovum. Its constituents are utilized by the ovum to build from its own structure a new organism, the embryo. At first this is always female, not sexually neutral as was formerly believed. In dissolving and transforming, the feminine is itself transformed. Although outwardly the feminine receives and submits to aggressive penetration, in the inner invisible mystery of her being she actively dissolves and dismembers in order to recreate, whereas the outwardly aggressive male, in this inner sanctuary, experiences the bliss of surrender to a different kind of wisdom. (p.136-37)

Thus we have a biological and psychological model that can be used as a guide for the formation of society—a society based upon a constant balancing and universal interchange of male/ female energy.

Many social scientists who argue for conformity and equality for men and women try to convince us that the differences between the sexes, both physical and mental, including most of the so-called typical sexual behavior traits, are actually just programmed by society. There is a grain of truth in this view but it is a view that ignores the obvious. Men and women are different! This difference extends to the very core of the natural and physical world and has its base in a metaphysical reality. One's sexuality is the foundation of one's identity and dictates a different way of being in and viewing the world. The levelling process, called equal rights for men and women, has so far produced an intensification of competitiveness between the sexes, a spread of homosexuality, an alienation and loneliness in both sexes, together with increased hostility and misunderstanding. In many cases, it produces a pathetic imitation or usurping of the standardized sex roles of one sex by the other. All attempts to neutralize or obscure the dynamic differences between male and female contribute to the degeneration of the vitality of humanity.

Jesse Jackson: Stirrings of a New Matriarchy

With the advent of Jesse Jackson in American politics, came a revived enthusiasm for egalitarian social ideals. Reverend Jackson's inspiring speeches are characterized by a mantra-like repetition of the goal of equality for all minority groups. Jackson images a Promised Land—a perfected, absolutely equalized, multiracial society. Jackson's phenomenal rise to political power is of particular interest to this discussion because the American black originated, relatively recently, from an indigenous tribal society—in other words, blacks carry with them the consciousness of an Earth-honoring matriarchal culture.* The tribal background represents, perhaps more than skin color, a greater estrangement from the patriarchal system, which initially considered blacks and all indigenous people as less than human. Present day black influence has helped to soften, sensualize, and physicalize American patriarchy. Generally, white society reacted to the release of black energy, image, and music by using more physical metaphor in language, becoming more rhythmic, more introspective, intuitive, immediate, informal, more carnal, and generally more "laid back." All these characteristics are reflective of the Universal Feminine and are those that would be expected to arise during the matriarchal phases of evolution. These changes have made contemporary America more humane, but they have not profoundly transformed the structure or course of patriarchal society. Like so many other recent innovative social movements—health and fitness, Eastern spirituality, environmental idealism—impetus by blacks for social transformation has failed, and instead, they have all been absorbed into the establishment, modifying its course. These indications, nonetheless, are perhaps embryonic stirrings of the coming matriarchal age.

Jackson, himself, reflects these same patterns: he has in many ways succumbed to an established social order, which is the antithesis of his blood instincts. He has become a fundamentalist Christian, with all the absolute, puritanical qualities of the patriarchal mindset. His children are all achievers in estab-

---

*The American Indians (Native Americans) are actually the indigenous tribal people of America but, because they were so crushed by the colonization of America, the African Blacks were able to carry more of the tribal matriarchal influences into American society.

lishment schools and careers. Jackson, as with most of us, is ensnared in an egalitarian system that imposes assimilation into a standardized mould in exchange for equal opportunities. Assimilation into the patriarchal system (the "American Way") means a surrendering, perhaps over several generations, of one's inherited cultural identity. It is conceivable that a multiracial society will advance beyond the present "melting pot" mentality. What is needed is a society that represents and maintains differences: genetic, linguistic, cultural, and instinctive. Again, the oldest existing matriarchal culture, the Australian Aborigine, provides a guiding model. These diverse aboriginal tribes carried out elaborate systems of exchange and interaction without violating the integrity of one another's territory, ancestral blood line, or linguistic and ritual practices. Matriarchy can encompass and sustain diversity without imposing assimilation because of its integral relationship with the environment. Patriarchy means colonization on every level: geographic, cultural, and psychological. The blacks, while modifying patriarchy, are themselves being colonized by it. Jackson aspires for equal opportunity to participate in an economic system based upon the model of colonization. Materialism, like colonization, is obsessed with acquisition and possession at the expense of one's competitor or victim. But the real loser is the Earth itself, which is antithetical to the Earth-honoring tribal traditions of Jackson's early ancestry. Tribal cultures such as the Australian Aborigines would never forcibly annex land belonging to another tribe; nothing is more sacred than the relationship of humanity to Mother Earth. Upon death, one's spirit enters a geographic feature of the local environment—trees, rocky out-crops, water holes, etc. The earth is pregnant with the spirit of its ancestors. For the Aborigine, humanity's dream of immortality can extend no further than the mortality of the earth.

> No Aboriginal could conceive that the world was in any way imperfect or incomplete. His religious life had a single aim—to keep the land the way it was in the beginning. To wound the earth is to wound yourself and if others wound the earth, they are wounding you. The land should be left untouched as it was in the Dreamtime when the Ancestors sang the world into existence. (Bruce Chatwin, *Songlines* p.54)

Alienation from the true nature and spirit of the Earth has caused people of all races to become alienated from the true nature of humanity. Significant change can only occur when blacks, whites and all races trapped in the present social paradigm accept that the leveling-off pressures in an egalitarian society force a standardized image of success upon all types of people and deny an identification of individual people with the universal image of their collective type. The laborer, the farmer, the merchant, the soldier, the aristocrat, the professional, the clergy, and the academic, all have an indispensable value and integral dignity in a social order. The pressures of open competition and upward mobility in materialistic, egalitarian societies place a burden, particularly on men, who are socially programmed to believe they must climb above their given status. The work a man does is of vital importance to his self-esteem and his feeling of well being, and therefore his sexual energy. The alienation and frustration that men have suffered as wage slaves and automats in the commercial, industrial and technological world is the bleak ever-present backdrop to the contemporary sexual crisis. The seed comes before the tree, and sexual relationships are the seed form upon which society is based. I believe therefore that Reich was correct when, after becoming disillusioned with Socialism, he proposed that humanity will liberate itself, not through abstract social doctrines, but by regaining the spiritual release and natural truth of sexual energy. Human society, including its relationship to planet Earth, will begin to transform only in relationship to the evolution of a new sexuality.

14·

The Chemistry of Sexual and Social Reformation

Almost all substances that we ingest chemically affect, to a greater or lesser degree, our perception and reaction to the world around us. There are substances, though, that more directly affect the neurotransmitters in the brain. These are called psychoactive substances, and components of these are often found in our everday foods. For example, if a nursing woman eats plenty of fresh salads and green vegetables, her lactation glands will concentrate a tranquilizing, morphine-like substance that, through her milk, will be passed to the feeding baby. Cow's milk is laced with this calming, morphine-like consciousness altering substance, because cows eat such vast quantities of green grass. Therefore, our association with mind-altering drugs starts at the very beginning of life and it is an association we share with every living species. From birds to bacteria, all species instinctively imbibe substances that get them "high" or drugged.[25] Not only drugs, but every edible food can have either constructive or destructive effects, depending on the amount used.

Social Disintegration: Sex and Drugs

Given the awareness that both food and drugs affect our consciousness and behavior, it is interesting to examine those substances that our patriarchal society on the one hand condones and on the other forbids. A pattern emerges, revealing that the acceptable substances accentuate the human characteristics valued by this society. Two common legitimate drugs in our society, tobacco and alcohol, are both psychoactive and highly destructive. It is interesting that these substances, so casually and routinely used today, were originally used only in religious ritual. Alcohol was consumed in religious ceremonies among early Middle Eastern cultures, and tobacco, among the indigenous people of North and South America where it was, and in some cases still is, used in witchcraft, as a ritual element in prayer, and in black magic.[26] In addition to the widely known carcinogenic effects of tobacco and its serious implications in heart disease, nicotine, along with the tropane alkaloids present in all plants of the tobacco family, have a direct negative effect on sexual energy and its development, particularly in males. Nicotine is one of the most toxic stimulants. If an ordinary cigar is soaked in a glass of water until the water becomes dark brown, the liquid contains enough poison to almost instantly kill two human beings. The toxins in tobacco are so strong that the body immediately sets up a tolerance reaction to it, within a matter of hours.[27] That tolerance reaction diminishes the ability of the nervous system to sensually respond and eventually lowers the production of sperm as well as of all the sex hormones.

The nicotine in cigarettes is a vasoconstrictor—that is, it constricts blood flow. A study by the United States Government found that men who smoked the equivalent of five cigarettes had a reduced amount of blood flowing to their penis during sexual arousal. Their erections were correspondingly smaller and lasted for a shorter time. Fertility is certainly affected by smoking cigarettes, as the restriction of blood to the male genitals also reduces sperm production. Smoking has the same affect on the genitals as it has on the coronary arteries.

It is interesting that many people become involved with tobacco during adolescence, that is during the period when our society imposes hypocritical restrictions on the expression of sexuality. Adolescence in both males and females is perhaps the most highly sexualized phase of life and adolescents may unconsciously adopt smoking as a way of diminishing their sexuality, to conform to the repressions placed upon it. It was noted in a study by the British Government that tobacco is particularly addictive among adolescents. An adolescent who has smoked even one pack of cigarettes has only a 15 percent chance of ever again becoming a nonsmoker.[28] In other societies in which adolescent sexuality is not repressed, there are no such incidences of self-destructive adolescent delinquency problems related to drinking, tobacco, and drugs. In effect, adolescents may be destroying their health or themselves in an attempt to destroy their sexuality, which finds no real acceptance or outlet within our society. Reich fought most of his life to try to bring about some sort of reasonable sexual expression for adolescents. He felt that the obstruction of adolescent sexuality is the primary reason that so many adults continue to live psychologically in the patterns and traumas of their childhood.

Some plants of the tobacco family enjoy a widespread use peculiar to modern civilization. This family of plants is called the *Solanaceous* or nightshade family and includes belladonna, henbane, mandrake and datura, all of which contain psychoactive chemicals called tropane alkaloids. Also in this family are common foods such as potatoes and tomatoes, which also contain these alkaloids to a much lesser degree but which, when concentrated, become a deadly poison. Generally, these tropanes block neurotransmission in the parasympathetic nervous system, reducing sensual responses while creating an anxiety syndrome of rapid heart rate, pupil dilation, dryness of skin, and flushing. In males the tropanes interfere with erection and ejaculation. A stronger member of the same family, belladonna, contributes to a gradual loss of sight. Datura creates an almost complete amnesia and a delirium that blocks awareness of physical sensation completely. Tobacco, before tolerance develops, also creates a delirium and a detachment from physical awareness. Its oldest use is in the American Indian ceremony of sweat lodges. Tobacco was used by the participants in the ceremonies to rise above the pain caused by exposure to scalding temperatures within a small enclosed space of the lodge. This again shows the physically detaching effect of this drug.

Alcohol is also an extremely toxic substance. When used in discreet amounts, or used ritualistically, it can reduce inhibitions, dispel worry and anxiety, and be conducive to social and sexual freedom. In larger doses its effect is just the opposite. It becomes completely debilitating, depressing the nervous system, preventing erections and drastically interfering with sexual performance. Government studies confirm that persistent abuse of alcohol can lead to permanent impotence and sexual dysfunction, through damage to the nervous system and the hormonal changes associated with liver damage. Alcohol is a by-product of fermentation, which happens spontaneously throughout nature. Grapes and grains, from which wine and beers are produced, carry on their skin the yeast spores that transform them into alcoholic beverages. Human intervention, in the form of distillation and concentration, disrupts the natural fermentation processes and has increased the toxicity and the damaging effects of alcohol use. Wine is a substance sacred to Dionysus, the god of merriment, sexual abandonment, dance, pleasure, and celebration. However, he was also the god of destruction, depravity, and madness. These extremes and excesses are reflected in the nature of alcohol, and one must use this substance with the awareness that it contains potentialities that are both life stimulating and deadly. *Patriarchal society condones the profane use of ritual substances which, when used habitually, diminish and deplete sexual and spiritual potential and destroy the physical and sensual responses of the nervous system.*

The recent Olympic drug scandals caricature the travesty of substance abuse utilized to support patriarchal competitiveness and its striving for standardized perfection. The young athletes, drugged on steroids and the mythic image of the warrior hero, are deluded into sacrificing their health and natural sexuality to the illusionistic goal of winning on the battle field of politicized sport. Ironically, multinational business interests pick up the media profits from these artificially stimulated, nearly superhuman exertions, while, at the same time, the Olympic Committee punishes the athletes for using the very substances that allow them to tolerate and achieve under the enormous competitive pressure.

The use of drugs touches upon a more far-reaching issue. Why does a substance in our outer environment have a direct, consistent effect on an inner subjective state of consciousness? The answer remains a mystery. An ancient theory recently reemerged in the morphogenetic field theory of modern biology: the primary shapes of molecules are in direct resonance with subtle energy fields that surround all substance, just as the shape and size of a wind pipe or a stretched cord has an association with consistent vibratory sound. The states of being that we experience—mental, emotional, and psychic—depend on a constant competition between molecules for positions on the synaptic nerve endings. This molecular war, which we become aware of and can partly control through our substance intake, exercise, etc., is a factor in the journey toward mastering our own consciousness. But this molecular condition of the body also reflects the condition of the energetic components associated with the formative forces surrounding all substance.

In *While the Gods Play*, Alain Danielou described this condition:

The states of our soul are due to the contingencies of a sort of war between armies of molecules corresponding to subtle beings. The aggression of one of these chemical spirits upon the human being is no different from that of a demon or an angel. It is a sort of possession. This is why a drugged person is no longer master of himself. He may detest the drug that imposes itself upon him despite himself. There exists a spirit of tobacco, a spirit of hemp, a spirit of peyote, a spirit of the poppy, a spirit of wine, which, if they are not controlled, lead their victim as they fancy. All religions have recognized the existence of these subtle forces and have sought to cajole them. (p.140-41)

The irrational and ignorant use of powerful intoxicating substances, which is contributing to the degeneration of the human species and the destruction of our sexuality, is part of a vast battle of opposing forces that rage inside the psyche of every individual as well as in the universe itself. It has been called "the battle of darkness and ignorance against light and truth," or the battle of evil against good, or cruelty against beauty. Whatever its name, it is the struggle to balance opposing forces, which underlie all of life and creation. In Greek thought this battle was designated the battle of Eros versus Thanatos. Eros was the god of life, loving, self-perpetuating forces, sexuality, pleasure, and creativity. Thanatos was the god of self-destruction, repression, diminution, and death. Both these forces are active in the universe and within our own consciousness. Our means of activating, controlling, or extending these energies is through our sexuality. It is through sexuality that we participate in the fundamental nature of creation. In a Shaivite text called *Shankara Digvijaya* (XV, 28) it says:

The state of ecstasy which manifests in the sexual act is a participation in the very nature of creation (*Bhairava*). What we call liberation (*moksha*) is the achievement of a state of ecstasy. Liberation is comparable to a permanent orgasm, an active state of delight (*ananda*) which is a part of the nature of the gods. He who venerates the self, established in the vulva (*Bhagasanastha*), attains liberation. (*Agama-Pramanya*). (p.141-42)

One could say that the moment the balance is broken—between the lifeforce, Eros, and the death drive, Thanatos, within the individual or within society—there is an inexorable slide toward unconscious self-destruction on every level. This self-destructiveness in part underlies the irrational use of drugs in this final phase of the patriarchal-dominant social order. There is a relationship here to the equally mad stockpiling of armaments, as well as to the destruction of the life-supporting atmosphere, environment, and planet. The forces of decay and destruction (Thanatos) are unleashed initially within the human body (through ignorance about diet and exercise in general and the use of toxic substances, which carry the spirit of destruction). It is a scientific fact that our internal reaction to the carcinogenic and toxic components in tobacco, alcohol, and industrial pollutants is the same as our chemical reaction to nuclear radiation.[29] In other words, the internal destructive imbalance that humanity creates within its own body is then projected outward and manifested in our technology and in the world we create around us. Technology is an externalization of principles and potentials that exist within our own physical bodies and minds. All our external construction, inventions, and technology preexist within the human body: the internal combustion engine is unconsciously modelled on the burning of carbohydrates in our digestive system; our nervous system is basically electrical; computers are modelled on the brain; the invention of the lever, arches, and hydraulics are anticipated by structures in our bodies. These ideas provide a wider understanding for the seemingly incomprehensible self-destruction that we see in the world around us. We live in an era of a degenerating social order that is in the process of self-destructing, and we as individuals absorb the contagions of that universal movement.

Two points should be kept in mind:

1. This discussion is not meant to be only an anti-smoking, anti-drinking argument; it is meant to clarify how the spiritual or subtle energetic forces of destruction and creation (the ancient gods) battle within the molecular balance of our own bodies and minds and from there project influences into the world at large.

2. As well, I do not mean to say that these substances or the process of destruction itself are innately evil or to be avoided. On the contrary, they are a part of the cosmic plan: every luscious, ripe piece of fruit contains within it the chemistry that brings about its

own decomposition. During periods of transition such as this, it is important to recognize what belongs to the process of degeneration and what factors might possibly represent a regeneration.

The Sexuality of Chemicals and Consciousness

Some of the struggles we face in our desire for social change are mediated within the chemistry of our bodies. The chemistry of our brains, like everything else in creation, is sexualized. There are two distinct neurochemical systems that control our states of being: the amphetamine-like compounds and the opiate-like compounds that are produced naturally in the brain. The psychoactive substances that we ingest (including mother's milk) either activate or repress to some degree these two internal neurochemical systems. The amphetamines represent the *male* neurochemical system; they include PEA (phenylethylamines), norepinephrine, dopamine, and serotonin. These compounds stimulate, activate, agitate, and, in extreme cases, produce anxiety and panic. Serotonin is active and necessary for the functioning of the rational, calculating mind, in other words the male-dominant hemisphere. On the other hand, the opiate-like compound (opioids) represent the *feminine* neurochemical system. This range of brain chemicals creates calm, release, merging, bonding, receptivity, and, in extreme cases, lethargy and depression. The amphetamines create the attraction/repulsion reactions in the brain: that which draws together, that which pulls apart. The opiates cause the binding of that which is attracted or the isolation of things that repel, in other words, the chemistry of holding together or holding apart. Drugs which stimulate us sexually (aphrodisiacs) repress the male amphetamine-like functions, which are active only in the preliminary courtship phase. Aphrodisiacs, in particular, repress serotonin, thereby releasing us from the domination of the rational mind.

Our society, education, and lifestyle presently overstimulate the serotonin and amphetamine male function of the brain. Therefore aphrodisiacs of one sort or another are often necessary to escape the anxiety-ridden brain chemistry of the modern world. The opioids in the brain, as well as the aphrodisiacs, often contain the enzyme MAO (monoamine oxidase). This enzyme metabolizes the amphetamine chemistry of the brain, allowing the relaxation and blending states of mind conducive to sexual union. With aphrodisiacs, the brain falls under the sway of Aphrodite, goddess of love and ritual and mother of Eros. Once the rational, calculating energy of the brain is repressed, we can enter into the limbic system or inner brain, which contains all the ritual images of the gods upon which our external personality is based. (I recommend for further reading *The Magical and Ritual Use of Aphrodisiacs* by Richard Alan Miller.)[30]

A holistic way of contemplating why the same internal chemicals that cause our innermost moods, emotions, and intellectual states are also found in various plants and minerals in nature could be developed along the following lines: the formation of matter is based on the attraction and bonding of oppositely charged energies/particles (a sexual dynamic). The ways in which these fundamental particles (atoms, molecules, cells) merge and produce formations in both living and nonliving substance implies an intelligence. The most advanced modern physicists talk about the "memory" of an atom because these tiny submicroscopic particles form, maintain, and reform habitually, according to basic patterns peculiar to themselves. Besides memory, there are processes of recognition, selection, rejection, identity, communication, rectification, substitution, etc., observable on the most fundamental level of matter. These activities indicate an active intelligence. Many modern physicists propose the existence of an innate intelligence within all matter, without which matter could never form or persist. It is not surprising, therefore, that the chemicals associated with our innermost states of consciousness are present in the flowers, trees, crystals, and minerals around us. In his numerous books on psychoactive drugs, Dr. Andrew Weil insistently reminds us that the drugs themselves do not create our mental state or condition but only release and activate a natural potential in our nervous system. Very often these substances simply allow our nervous system to perceive the world in a different manner. Freudian psychology (a patriarchal concept), on the other hand, refuses to believe that the entire content of the unconscious—dreams, hallucinations, fantasies, visions—is anything other than an abstraction based on illusions or distortions of the mind straying from normalcy. But modern brain research enables us to see beyond this idea and understand that dreams, visions, etc. belong to the chemistry and function of the limbic system, the seat of the universal feminine intelligence. These states of awareness, out of which the myths of older civilizations arose, have their basis in a long-repressed natural activity of the brain and nervous system. The chemicals of perception in our brains, as well as those same chemicals found in plants and minerals (the mind of nature), allow us to perceive a purely energetic world associated with the formative energies (the spirit or intelligence) of each substance. Freudian psychology claims that all our subconscious distortions go back to our childhood experiences and traumas with our parents. It is now possible to assimilate the Freudian concept into a wider, more physically and spiritually integrated viewpoint: our parents are a given or foreordained element in our lives. Our relationship with them can be considered, as in Western genetics, as a result of the "accident of birth"—in Eastern psychology, the just fate or *karma* of an evolving soul. In either case, Mother and Father are the first archetypes that we encounter. They are as much representatives of the universal roles of creators and life-givers as they are the individual folks we know as mom and dad. Indeed, to the infant child, Mother and Father are like gods: powerful beings upon whom the fate of the tiny child depends. Our brain and body chemistry patterns are set by the creative/destructive archetypal energies represented to us through our parents. Once established, these patterns continue to determine our reaction and affinities to the outer world. They also determine in part what substances we take into our body and what phenomenal events we draw into our unfolding lives.

For example, if a female child has a mother who frequently inflicts physical punishment, this child will develop in her chemistry an affinity with the destructive inhumane and terrifying aspects of the universal mother—that aspect of Mother Nature that ultimately destroys everything in creation. This force, called Kali in Indian mythology, is the same force as that of Medea in the Greek myth. In adulthood, hormonal imbalances, due to these childhood beatings, may affect a woman's menstrual periods, causing depressions and powerful destructive urges, during which she would like to do away with everything including herself. The woman can break this childhood psychochemical bondage through introspection, self-awareness, analysis, and other self-disciplines that allow her to see these configurations, in a psychological (abstract) way and to change them in a chemical (physical) way. These disciplines have been the basis for the search for self in many psychospiritual traditions. The "hero" of this search must confront and conquer the dark aspect of the Mother and Father within the chemistry of his or her own mind. Thus, in addition to their genetic influence, parents can, through the violence or benevolence of their discipline, alter the child's brain chemistry. This chemical imbalance creates vulnerabilities and propensities related to the Freudian idea of childhood traumas, and it provides a physical explanation as to how they persist into adulthood. I have chosen a woman for this example because there is more clinical evidence on females for the way psychological or archetypal traumas inscribe themselves as metabolic imbalances than on males. Equally, male impotency, for example, could be cited as the chemical imprint left by the terrifying face of the dark aspect of Mother.

From a spiritual dimension, we understand that brain chemistry underlies and represents experiences of consciousness. That is to say, chemical configurations imply states of being that then have affinities, reactions, and repulsions with chemical states in others and with substances in the world around us. These universal states of being, which live and express themselves through our biochemistry, are none other than the gods of ancient times, and they have a chemical/energetic existence throughout nature as well as in the neuro-chemistry of perception. The existence of the gods is as real as any other aspect of the so-called normal perceivable world. In the patriarchal age, we have repressed the use and cultivation of that aspect of our brain and nervous system through which the gods can enter our sense of reality.

These thoughts can be considered as part of an emerging new paradigm in human psychology—which integrates all levels of experience from metaphysics to molecules. The polarity dynamic of attraction/repulsion, which is basic to the formation of matter, is an activity of universal consciousness which, like our own human consciousness, is sexualized. With this understanding, it is possible to discover the parallel between our psychological and physical states. We can also discover that parallel in the metaphysical principles that preside over all the processes of mind and matter.

15·

Generation/Degeneration

One of the problems weighing on the Earth's future and on the future of sexuality is our immensely swollen population. The pressure of feeding, clothing, and housing such huge numbers makes unthinkable any idea of fundamentally altering the present socioeconomic organization. In fact, it seems we are chained to a system that, if left unchanged, will reduce most of the earth and its atmosphere to a desert within two or three generations. The population problem is undeniably linked to our ideas about sexuality. But overpopulation cannot be alleviated by patriarchal sexual repression, as recent centuries have shown. There are, however, some possible solutions associated with matriarchal psychology and forms of knowledge.

First, anthropologists and scientific researchers are discovering that indigenous, so-called primitive cultures have the knowledge of numerous methods and substances that act as natural contraceptives. Research into understanding these procedures and regaining the use of many of these esoteric herbs and substances could give us contraceptive alternatives to the synthesized Pill which, along with fertility, destroys the subtle physical mechanisms that enhance the attractiveness of women to men.

Second, since Greek times, patriarchal society has minimized the number of archetypal images and models from which women could extract a broader sense of their identity as individuals. From the Greek pantheon of goddesses, the Western Christian world elevated only those female images that are dependent on relationships with men. These were Demeter, the goddess of motherhood, Hera, the goddess of domesticity and the household, Venus/Aphrodite, the alluring and beautiful sexual object, Persephone, the eternal innocent daughter, etc. Prior to Greek civilization, women, especially in Indian society, had archetypal models that were completely independent of relationships with men and the roles and duties of procreation. There are goddesses such as Lakshmi, the archetype of the woman artist, dancer, poetess, musician, who never dreamed of marriage, domesticity, or children.[31] The esteemed temple courtesans studied the erotic sciences and had a full sexuality, related to spiritual growth. There were also Greek images like the goddess, Artemis, who was a chaste, solitary, independent wanderer and huntress of the wilderness, or Sophia, the goddess of female wisdom and philosophy, who never involved herself in the procreative function. Many modern women have been forced to find their identities only in relationship to the childbearing, male-dependent models of femininity. All other lifestyles in modern society are implicitly deemed unnatural. There are undoubtedly vast numbers of women involved in these domestic, maternal roles, who are in conflict with an inner voice that hungers for some other model to guide their lives. Quite simply, all women are not meant for procreation, and this forcing of feminine nature into the maternal mode is another factor contributing to the constant rise in population.[32] Some women now should become free to seek an active identity with feminine archetypes other than those dominated by procreation and domesticity and devote their creative energy to the insurrection, struggle, and transformation necessary to save the planet from destruction.

The third factor that can affect population is something we have dealt with thoroughly in another context: the cultivation of male sexuality and the technique of sperm retention. Implementing this practice would contribute enormously to solving the problem of unwanted babies; it would also further the evolution of the ritualistic and spiritual potentials of human sexuality.

These solutions to the population explosion have little effect on another obstruction to the evolution of human sexuality: sexually transmitted diseases, such as AIDS. However, a metaphysical overview will give us a more holistic perspective on this devastating problem. It is scientifically evident that sexuality is not the cause of AIDS but the most obvious and effective method of transmission. It is a disease that seriously undermines our psychological attitudes towards sexuality, just at a critical moment in the evolution of Western sexual values. Granted the so-called sexual revolution of the 1960s had many confusions and pitfalls. But it did release vast numbers of people into an acceptance, appreciation, and enjoyment of the physical body and its erotic functions. The recent health and fitness movement, with its new dietary awareness, is a by-product of the sexual revolution and has, in the past fifteen years, contributed to a significant reduction in heart disease in America. With all its flaws, the sexual revolution of the 1960s helped to sweep away a millennium of repressive dogmas and attitudes. We finally faced the fact that "what is natural cannot be evil." The 1980s have brought new problems and, while it is necessary to adopt precautionary attitudes toward hygiene and promiscuity, it is equally important not to allow the AIDS scare to diminish our evolution toward greater physical awareness and sexual appreciation.

It will soon be understood that the cause of the AIDS epidemic must be laid at the doorstep of a much more complex matter than modern promiscuity. The roots of its cause probably lie with the relationship of industrial civilization (masculine) to the ecology of the earth (feminine). The breakdown of the immune system in individual people is parallel to that of the breakdown of the ozone layer of the atmosphere. Certainly, the ozone layer in relation to the body of the planet functions in a way similar to our immunological responses: filtering out harmful radiation as our immune system filters out harmful cells. It is possible that the changes in the quality of light transmitted by our ozone-reduced atmosphere are responsible for alterations and mutations in viruses, creating new strains that our immune systems, already overburdened from industrial pollutants and improper diet, cannot fight. During the present patriarchal dominant stage of history, we have forgotten the old matriarchal awareness that we are an inseparable part of this earth. A sick biosphere and an unhealthy earth can only lead to a sick and declining humanity.

Metaphysically, then, AIDS may relate to the imbalance between the aggressive thrust of civilization (male) and the receptive, containing environment of the earth (female). This in turn reflects the imbalances of male and female energy within our society and within ourselves as individuals. Therefore the key to the regeneration of our relationship with Planet Earth lies in the harmonization of masculinity and femininity within individual men and women. The sexual polarity in us is our direct access to the fundamental polarity that governs nature and underlies all creation. It is for this reason that sexuality is the key, not only to our physical and psychological health, but to our spiritual health. No longer relevant is the emphasis, in this passing patriarchal age, on monasticism, celibacy, and withdrawal from the vital and physical aspects of life for the purpose of spiritual growth. The hope for the new age, the regeneration of individuals, the species, and the environment, will only be found through an understanding and reshaping of sexuality.

16·

Sexuality
and the Universe Evolving

The pervasiveness of bioclocks in living systems gives us a sturdy empirical metaphor upon which to expand a psychology based on the interrelatedness of our minds with the universe. Over twenty years of research in the field of biorythms demonstrates that the metabolic processes in living organisms are geared to regular movements of the sun, the moon, and the planets in relation to the earth. These movements include the rotation of the earth upon its axis, the earth's revolution around the sun, and the moon's encircling of the earth. Indeed, it is presently believed that there is no bodily process that does not exhibit cyclic variations: that all organisms on earth contain metabolic clocks which, at apportioned intervals related to geo-celestial cycles, trigger essential internal biological activities.[33]

The most obvious bodily cycle dependent upon the position and radiation of the sun and moon is the sexual fertility/dormancy cycle. Using the thought pattern of macrocosm/microcosm—as above/so below—we can expand the yearly oscillation between the fertility/dormancy patterns as a model for the matriarchal/patriarchal patterns that we have used to describe the five-thousand-year oscillation of history.

Approximately five thousand years ago, the older Neolithic matriarchal societies began to give way to conquering patriarchal societies. The matriarchal period of historical expression was one in which humanity existed in a heightened attunement to nature and natural progressions and cycles. The human organism possessed an extreme sensitivity to electromagnetic and subtle life currents flowing through the earth, the atmosphere, indeed through all substance living and non-living. During the matriarchy, human beings cultivated these sensitivities and lived and behaved as an embodied expression of the patterns, laws, and energetic principles contained in the earth and sky. Humankind was the perfect child of Mother Nature. During this period, humans relied much less on the reasoning, decision-making, rational mind (corresponding to the cerebral cortex or "male" mind, and the voluntary nervous system). Human life and intelligence were dominated by the receptive, sensitized, intuitive mind (corresponding to the ancient parts of the brain called the limbic system, the "female" mind, and the autonomic nervous system).

In the older region of the brain is found the mysterious pineal gland, which picks up and responds to subtle magnetic and electric currents from the earth, rocks, trees, and other animals and humans, as well those electromagnetic currents in the air, clouds, dew, and rain. These subtle energy currents of earth and sky are affected by the sun, the moon, the position of the planets and even, perhaps, more distant cosmic radiation. Modern scientific equipment now verifies the presence of these energies and the capacity for organisms to respond to them. The older, deeper brain (the limbic system) houses glands such as the thalamus and hypothalamus, which are active in creating moods and states of mind, including all the "primitive" emotional responses: anger, fear, affection. Also there is the master gland, the pituitary, which activates the higher emotional responses of joy, ecstasy, awe, and love. Contained also in the limbic system is the brain structure called the hippocampus, which is involved in the memory related to the physical body and deeply held sensations of pain and pleasure. The limbic system within the forebrain contains all the ritual behavior of courtship, territorial aggression, etc., which reaches back to reptilian forms of life. It also contains the centers related to the erotic excitement of sexual experience rather than the reproductive function.[34] The limbic system contains the characteristics that we associate with universal femininity: it is receptive, sensual, and feeling. Its activities suffuse our life with the energies of the earth and the environment around us; its glands nourish and regulate the entire body, including the instinctive/intuitive intellect. During the matriarchal phases of evolution, this brain function was primary. Humanity lived naked in the natural world: bare feet were pressed against the earth; eyes, chest, skin, and genitals were open and sensitive to light and air, veritable receiving stations for movements of earthly and cosmic energies. This phase of our evolution is the Garden of Eden or paradise alluded to in numerous ancient texts. This primal state was probably last seen completely intact before the British invaded, and almost completely destroyed, the Aboriginal culture of Australia.

The growth of the cerebral cortex is perhaps one of the most accelerated developments in biological evolution. All its manifold functions are reminiscent of those characteristics that we associate with universal masculinity and the patriarchal order. The cerebral cortex accepts only perceptions and sensations that have first been repressed and filtered; in other words, it accepts only a selective amount of information. It is like the Universal Masculine, in that it selects and constructs its own reality, rather than receiving and harmonizing with a greater reality. The cerebral cortex is involved with the recognition and expression of language and symbols: it reduces, simplifies, manipulates, and calculates. This capacity to filter, repress, and construct allows the cerebral cortex to see reality as something external and separate from itself. This is a perception mode basic to the psychology of an independent, isolated identity and is therefore the source of sensing ourselves as individuals.

The ability to objectify gives rise to the capacity to think and comprehend in the abstract. For example, the endless flow of time is abstracted into past, present, and future. These abstractions of time and space in turn give rise to a sense of separation from the past, along with the imagination and anticipation of a definite future. Both these energies of isolation and anticipation generate the experience of anxiety and worry, which tend to exhaust the energy reserves of the sensual and feeling levels of perception.

Thus we see in the evolution of two distinct areas of the brain a contrast of the same characteristics associated with the Universal Feminine and the Universal Masculine. It is as if the oscillation or copulation between these two metaphysical forces of gender generates distinctly different phases in the unfolding of history. I think this idea could provide a clearer understanding of the larger movements of history than the Darwinian concept of a linear progression provides. The shape of historical time may not be a straight line but an ever-recurring spiral. In other words, we needn't interpret the emergence of the cerebral cortex as some sort of permanent progress or evolutionary transcendence over the functionings of the inner regions of the brain. We can see each region as complementary, with each achieving a predominance in some sort of recurring oscillation throughout evolution. The evolution of the internal brain's function is not yet complete, nor is its integration with the external cerebral cortex. This work may be the content of future chapters in human evolution.

We can discover, in the function of our brain, how patriarchal energy imprinted its power and dominance. To the degree that we change our environment, we also change ourselves. Patriarchal society has continually constructed architectural environments that cut humanity off from the natural environment. We now live in tombs of concrete and glass. Rubber-soled shoes and thick pavements block the flow of the earth energies to our feet and nervous system. Walls of glass and stone cut us off day after day from natural sunlight, as well as from the luminosities of night. A blanket of pollutants and artificially generated electromagnetic fields cut us off from the influx of energy from the solar system and beyond. In this thick cocoon humanity stands, isolated from the earthly and celestial energies that connect us to nature and the world around us. All the photosensitive glands and neurons of the limbic system are starved of the stimuli and signals from light and the atmosphere. It is no wonder, then, that we are

DIAGRAM 7. THE EVOLUTION OF THE HUMAN BRAIN

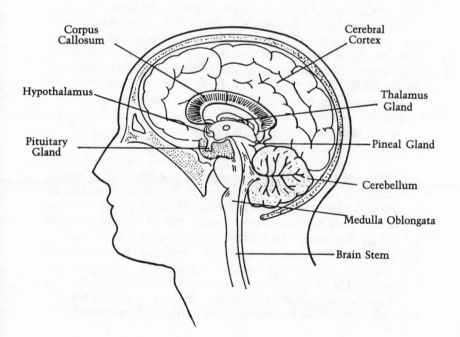

Corpus Callosum

Cerebral Cortex

Hypothalamus

Thalamus Gland

Pituitary Gland

Pineal Gland

Cerebellum

Medulla Oblongata

Brain Stem

pushed to excessive dependence on the qualities of mind that originate from the male-dominant modes of the cerebral cortex. Instead of moving instinctively and intuitively in tune with the seasons of time and the rhythms of nature, we conceive of ourselves as making rational, self-motivated decisions, ignorant of the energies and forces that connect us to a larger whole. In John Lennon's words, "Life is something that happens to you while you're busy making other plans."

We can find in both ancient philosophy and modern science indications of how our bodies regulate energies received from the earth and the sky. It is not the male cerebral cortex, but the feminine inner brain that controls our sexuality as well as our subtle responses to the environment. The surmounting "male" cerebral cortex can be allegorically related to the Sky, whose energies direct the intentional movement and will of organisms on Earth, while the "female" limbic inner brain corresponds to the receiving, reacting Earth. This view of sexuality, based on modern brain research, was held centuries ago by a Taoist master named Tung. Here is a translation from his ancient Taoist text in *Sexual Secrets*:

> Of all things that make mankind prosper, none can be compared to sexual intercourse. It is modelled after Heaven and takes its form by Earth; it regulates Yin and rules Yang. Those who understand its significance can nurture their nature and prolong their years. But those foolish people, or societies, who cannot understand its true significance harm themselves and die before their time. Truly, Heaven revolves to the left and earth revolves to the right. Thus the four seasons succeed each other; man thrusts, woman receives; above there is action, below compliance. (p. 266)

This Taoist image, while supporting the Earth/female:Sky/male analogy, suggests male dominance. In contrast, Tantric images from the same period place the female, symbolically, on top of the male during intercourse, a view that is also maintained in the Egyptian Earth/Sky image of Nut and Geb (see Appendix). The harmonic principle discussed in Chapter 7 helps untangle the discrepancy between these Taoist and Tantric images. Harmony occurs because the relationship between opposites always exits concurrent with it's reciprocal inversion; *male/female=female/male*. From the point of view of Earth, the Universal Feminine principle should dominate. The feminine, in most ancient and tribal cultures, is viewed as the proper power and authority to govern earthly life, human society, and material organization in general, while the proper domain of male authority and power is in spiritual and metaphysical concerns. The masculine principle maintains the rituals and structures that connect life to the unmanifest forces and through men these forces guide and animate the feminine domain. This organizational concept explains why male sexuality should naturally be oriented toward control, mastery, and transcendence of the physical aspects of drive and release. Masculinity, through ritual, maintains the connection to the past order and to the great plan at the origin of creation. Women, reciprocally, in ritual or sexual abandonment of their innate earthly connnectiveness (Nut in the Sky), provide the psychic space in which men can forgo their innate sense of metaphysical separateness and experience groundness and relationship with life as it is, (Geb on Earth). According to the philosophy of Earth-Mother cultures, human evolution falters and degenerates when this harmonic inversion is broken. Western civilization inherited, and then ignored, a way of thinking similar to Taoist and tribal thought with the Greek philosopher Empedocles, who was excommunicated from Pythagorean Mystery School for committing this most ancient oral teaching to writing. Basic to this tradition was the classification of contrasting objects or qualities in pairs. Each binary set generates basic related qualities, for example:

Earth	Sky
Female	Male
Water	Fire
Body	Mind
Mother	Father
Substance	Radiation

With these correspondences in mind, we can consider a world cosmology of origins according to an Earth-Mother (geocentric universe) that is, in every way, opposite to the patriarchal assumptions (solar system, Big Bang) we accept as reality. According to the perception of the Earth-Mother, the Earth is the center of the universe. All the stars, the sun, and the moon, the glistening, radiant bodies of the sky, were projected from the earth, just as our thoughts and mental activities are projections reflecting the internal states of organs and bodily energies. The body is the womb of the mind, just as the earth is the womb of the universe.* Christ, the Sun King, is born from the Black Virgin. The molten fire within the belly of Earth is projected outward to become the Sun. All of existence is the projection outward of internal, subjective states into objective ideas, forms, and substances: the Sky is the "dreaming" of the Earth. All life and all energies emerge from the Earth, even those that we consider subtle and celestial. There is a constant exchange between the Earth and its dreaming. The stars in the sky are the spirit energy of beings who were born from, and who have lived on, Earth, just as all men emerge into the world from the female womb. These ancestral beings return from the dreaming (the starry firmament) as radiated light and heat, which generate new life on Earth. The male sperm is analogous to this radiation as it fertilizes the female but, itself, was born from the female. Our minds and imaginations are always attempting to listen to the voice returning from the starry ancestors and we then reimage them. The Earth also listens to the returning ancestral energies and may reincarnate them. All creation occurred from Earth and all recreation occurs through her. There is nothing more than Earth, the Universal Female, and its dreaming, the Universal Male.

---

*By implication, modern theoretical physics has revived the validity of the Earth-centered universe in acknowledging that the existence of the universe is inseparable from, and dependent upon, the living consciousness of that which perceives it. We observe the universe from the center of life through the perception of the Earth. No one, not even a satellite, has observed a sun-centered solar-system, as every celestial body moves around every other.

APPENDIX

Every universal path approaches becoming a circle, that then opens into the unknown. Circular movement reflects and maintains a dynamic constancy of opposites. Every point on a circular curve relates to an opposite yet equal point. Opposite points on a circle are the same, yet different: are complementary, yet antagonistic. The beginning, ending, and rebeginning converge as a unity of three. Beginning and ending are nearly aligned, yet never quite identical. The past and future: the way forward and the way back, reflect each other like a mirror image, identical yet inverse. (See Diagram 8.)

I believe human society is located, inevitably, on the ever-changing curvature between proceeding forward and turning back. The further back into the past that we can look, the more likely we shall be able to recognize our destiny.

For those who are already familiar with ancient cosmology and the theory of cycles and history, it is interesting to compare the general model of alternation between patriarchy and matriarchy, with the ancient Hindu theory of time and history.

The Hindu scriptures divide the world cycle into four different ages or *yugas*. The first age is the Krita Yuga, which means the Golden Age, considered to be the Paradise or Garden of Eden remembered in so many ancient mythologies. It is followed by Treta Yuga, which literally means the Cycle of Three (Fires), referring to a phase in civilization that ritually remembers the preceding Golden era. Next is Dvapara Yuga, which literally means the Age of Doubt and Uncertainty. In this yuga, the cosmic harmony between heaven and earth is disrupted and man has to live, alienated in the earthly environment, by his wits and resources. "Man loses a sense of the divine reality of the world and grows away from the natural law" (Alain Danielou, *While the Gods Play*). The last or present age is Kali Yuga, which means the Age of Darkness and Conflict.

The word *Cain* in Hebrew comes from the same root as the word *Kali* in Sanskrit. The Hebrew verb *Kanna*, like the Sanskrit equivalent, means to count, to calculate, to acquire, to own, to subjugate. In his book *The Songlines*, Bruce Chatwin notes that:

> "*Cain* also means metalsmith. Since, in several
> languages—even Chinese—the words for *violence*
> and *subjugation* are linked to the discovery of metal,
> it is perhaps the destiny of Cain and his descendants
> to practice the black arts of technology." (p.193)

In the Hindu tradition, the measuring stone of the cycles of time is called Kala and each of the first three ages is a multiple of Kali Yuga, the final or concluding age of darkness, which has a duration of 6,048.72 years. (The other three ages are successive multiples—2, 3, 4—of the number of years in Kali Yuga.)

According to the *Linga Purana* (1.4.3-6), "The relative duration of the four ages is, respectively, 4,3,2,1. Each age is preceded by a period of dawn and followed by a period of twilight. These

DIAGRAM 8. THE OPEN CIRCLE OF TIME

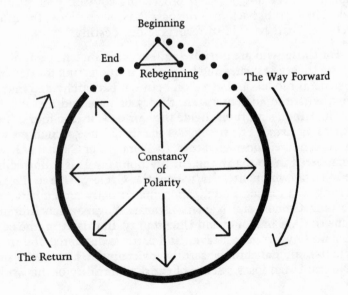

transition periods (amsha) at the beginning and end of each Yuga last a tenth of the duration of the Yuga."[1]

In While The Gods Play (p.96), Alain Danielou describes the entire scheme and the duration in years of the four yugas as follows:

The Golden Age	Dawn of Krita Yuga		2,016.24
	Krita Yuga		20,162.40
	Twilight		2,016.24
		Total:	24,194.88

The Age of Ritual	Dawn of Treta		1,512.10
	Treta		15,121.80
	Twilight		1,512.10
		Total	18,146.00

The Age of Doubt	Dawn of Dvapara		1,008.10
	Dvapara		10,081.20
	Twilight		1,008.10
		Total	12,097.40

The Age of Conflict and Darkness	Dawn of Kali		504.06
	Kali		5,040.60
	Twilight		504.06
		Total	6,048.72

The total of the four yuga(s) is 60,487 human years. This figure is approximately the time that the Australian Aborigines have maintained their primordial matriarchal culture.

In comparing this time system with my concept of the fluctuation of the Universal Masculine and Feminine, we can say that the first three yugas correspond to matriarchal Earth-Mother ages, totaling 54,438.28 years: the Golden Age (24,194.88 years) is the rise of Matriarchy to its ascendency, the two successive ages, Treta and Dvapara (18,146 and 12,097.40 years respectively), representing the declining stages of the matriarchal age of history. Approximately 5,000 years ago patriarchy begins to ascend.

There is a biological model supporting the idea of a three to one ratio between number of periods allotted to matriarchal dominance in relationship to male dominance. In the growth of a plant there are three phases in which growth and extension are continuous. They can be graphically labelled. The first stage produces the root system and stem or trunk. These are the longest or slowest growth functions in a tree and could be compared to the Golden Age. The next growth function is the branching and leafing, which is of a shorter duration and comparable to the Age of Ritual in the Hindu Cycle of Time. The third stage of growth is budding and flowering, again shorter than the second stage, and comparable to the Age of Doubt. In the fourth and final stage of the forming of the fruit and seed, the growth or extension of the plant stops and the entire lifeforce of the plant system is focused in the seed. This phase brings to conclusion the plant's season of growth and, as in Kali Yuga, the plant's energy degenerates and the information of its being is deposited in the seed. As we have indicated, Kali Yuga, amid all its degeneration and destruction, produces instances of heightened individuality: people who can be the transmitters of essence to reinstate the beginning of a new cycle.

According to the traditional Hindu calendar, Kali Yuga commenced in 3012 B.C., the middle of Kali Yuga is 582 B.C., the beginning of the twilight is A.D. 1939, and the end of the twilight of Kali Yuga is A.D. 2442. The imbalance of masculine energy (Kali Yuga) is the necessary phase of the destruction and decomposition of the old forms before the new forms emerge. The diagram would go as such:

DIAGRAM 9. THE YUGAS
AND THE PATRIARCHAL/MATRIARCHAL

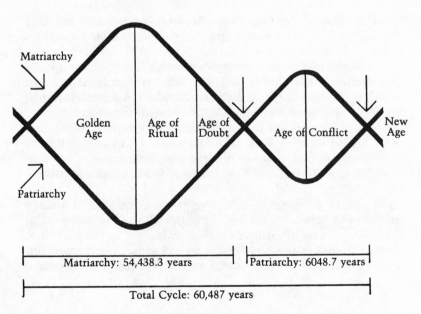

According to this scheme, the height of the patriarchal age, from about 650 B.C. to 500 B.C., shows the emergence of the great prophets of our period, along with the accomplishment of written alphabets. Greek and Phoenecian writing appears at this time, along with the lives of Zoroaster, Lao Tse, Confucius, Buddha, and Pythagoras. Also, the male-dominant civilization of Rome establishes itself as a Republic.

The clarification of Diagram 9 can be found in the well known Egyptian wall painting showing the separation of Nut, the Feminine Principle, from Geb, the Masculine Principle (see Diagram 10). This image supports our idea of the creative power being associated with the inversion of the male and female roles. The Feminine Principle, Nut, which is traditionally the earth, rises in an arch, as the vault of the Sky, while Geb, the Masculine Sky principle, lies on the ground staring at the Earth, as if becoming infused in it. *The ascendency of the Feminine Principle in the Golden Age is balanced by the Male Principle gaining its greatest depth of relatedness.* It is not meant to imply a domination or subjugation of the masculine by the feminine. In Kali Yuga, the male Sky Father ascends and the Earth Mother declines, breaking the balance of inversions. This is symbolized in same Egyptian image by the Divine Cow, which emphasizes the nutritive character of the cosmic environment. The hieroglyphs above the Divine Cow read, "Destruction to men when they revolt against the creative balance." The King or Pharaoh stands between the image of Nut and Geb, Earth and Sky, his arms held in the position of balancing. One could surmise that the entirety of the Egyptian spiritual legacy was a formalized remembrance and repository of the Golden Age of the preceding matriarchal phase of evolution.

One might detect a feminist superiority in allotting three ages to matriarchal dominance and only one to patriarchy. This, of course, has a biological basis in that the male sexual characteristic is only a single tag chromosome on the ubiquitous female genetic structure. The patriarchal creation myth has inverted the order of birth in saying that Eve was created from the side rib of Adam. In the ancient matriarchy, the creation of man resulted from the Eternal Mother taking a small portion of her swollen stomach (enlarged womb) and attaching it to the male to form his genitals. This sequence is reflected still in the roots of the words for man and woman and has subsisted even into modern English. The word *woman* is derived from "womb-man," in other words, men who have inscribed in their body and spirit the capacity to give birth and bring into the world new life. The word *man* represents "wombless-man" or men without wombs. One can also observe that the small amount of semen emitted from the male genitals is tiny and insignificant when compared with an entire infant, which emerges from the fe-

DIAGRAM 10. DETAIL OF THE GREENFIELD PAPYRUS

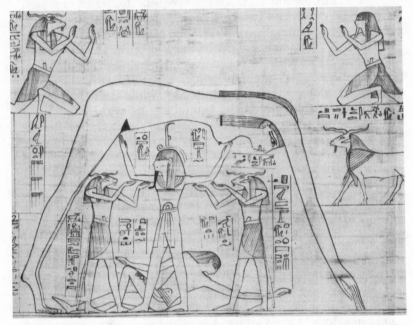

One key to understanding this enigmatic Egyptian symbol is the strange inversion of the male/female roles and positions. The male Sky Father Principle, Geb, is depicted as being held in Earth. This position symbolizes immanency, that is, the male godhead is seen and felt to be present and involved in the very core of nature and physical life. In contrast, the feminine Earth Mother Principle, Nut, is elevated to the Sky and adored as the preeminent principle of the universe. History marks the moment when the balancing of the inverted principles was broken "the time when the cult of the Sky-father began to replace the worship of the Earth-mother . . . apparently was when the Copper Bronze Age replaced the New Stone Age some 4000 to 5000 B.C. Thus, it is a rather apt statement to record, as history does, that the stone bowl was replaced by the copper cauldron" (Clyde E. Keeler, *Secrets of the Cuna Earth-Mother* p. 274).

male.[2] Hence the feminine principle is the dominant energy during the creative cycles of human evolution and the male principle ascends only for the necessary phase of dissolution preceding a new cycle of time.

EPILOGUE

Fortunately, there remain frail vestiges of ancient matriarchy-based, indigenous populations—battered, oppressed, and deprived after a millennia of colonization—scattered over the face of the earth. These cultures, of which the Australian Aborigines are the oldest and the most pure, may hold, with their mysterious traditions, the instructions for human survival. That survival undoubtedly depends on regaining the connective flow between humanity and earth. The legacy of these cultures is not to be copied and imitated in romantic reactionaryism, but rather their essences must be gleaned and translated into a paradigm for the future.

The problems that face our self-destructing world system are grave and manifold, but to blame, or feel remorse, or a sense of sin is useless. To initiate the vast changes necessary for human survival, we have at our disposal human sexual energy and its power to shape relationships both individual and social. Sexuality is the seed for the generation of all change: all food and nourishment comes from seeds, the source of all new life. Seed energy is like the "dreaming" of the future: it is both the source and the essence, not only of our physical, but of our spiritual nature. The original meaning of the word *sin* in Hebrew is "the wasting of seed", and this is why the cultivation of male sexuality, as we understand it in the light of research into both ancient and modern sources, can be a key for resuming our spiritual evolution.

Our present situation was summarized and symbolized for me during a flight on a tiny four-seater aircraft from Alice Springs to Ayres Rock in Central Australia. As the flight began, we crossed the McDonald Ranges, flying within miles of the maximum security American satellite-tracking installation called Pine Gap. In the distance, the metal balloon structures appeared like fragile clusters of enlarged mushrooms, tenuously imposed on the incomprehensibly vast expanse of the desert. The ominous high-technology enclosure represented a tent-like temple to the patriarchal Sky Father. The air was seeping out of these mushrooms of the dying Sky god: man's missile and space programs are floundering, world-wide computer systems are being infected with self-destructive program viruses; meanwhile, Mother Earth, with unprecedented force, presses for the transformation of human society with hurricanes, droughts, fires, floods, and heat waves.

After an hour's flight, Ayres Rock emerged in the distance like a huge, luminous, pulsating navel on the womb of the world. It was as if the plane had been swept into the presence of the most powerful of all Earth-Mother temples, standing as it has for four thousand million years. In the presence of this earthly architecture, one understands what the Aborigines here, and indigenous peoples elsewhere, have always known: man cannot own the land, the land owns mankind. As Yirralla in his book, *Australian Dreaming*, aptly states:

> We belong to the ground,
> It is our power and we
> must stay close to it or maybe,
> we will get lost.

REFERENCES

Introduction
1 Nahum Stiskin, *The Looking Glass God* (Tokyo: Weatherhill, 1972),
pp. 41–43.

Part 1: Sexuality and Self
1 Emma Jung, *Animus and Anima* (Zurich: Spring Publications, 1978),
pp. 9–11; 45–50.
2 David Boadella, *Willhelm Reich: The Evolution of His Works* (London: Arkana, 1985), pp. 18–19; 116–123.
3 Benjamin Walker, *Tantrism* (London: The Aquarian Press, 1985), pp.
10–18.

Chapter 1: The Heterosexual Options
4 Jo Durden-Smith and Diane de Simone, *Sex and the Brain* (London:
Pan Books, 1983), pp. 11–16.
5 *Time Magazine*, May 1988.
6 Smith and de Simone, *Sex and the Brain*, pp. 191–204.
7 Herb Goldberg, *The New Male-Female Relationship* (London: Coventure, 1984).
8 Warren Farrell, *Why Men Are the Way They Are* (New York: McGraw-Hill, 1986), pp. 113–121.
9 Goldberg, *The New Male-Female Relationship*.
10 Farrell, *Why Men Are the Way They Are*, pp. 124–141.
11 Daniel Walman, an acupuncturist and physiotherapist, in a verbal
interview with Robert Lawlor on his research into sex hormone
therapy.
12 Morris Berman, *The Reenchantment of the World* (New York: Bantam Books, 1984).
13 Sam Keen, *The Passionate Life: Stages of Loving* (London: Gateway
Books, 1985), pp. 10–15.

14 Bruce Holbrook, *The Stone Monkey* (New York: William Morrow & Co. Inc., 1981), pp. 61–68.
15 Smith and de Simone, *Sex and the Brain*, p. 105.

Chapter 2: Civilization, Sexuality and the Sacred
The source that reveal the sexual origins of present-day religious ceremony are extensive. These references are based on a study of Tantric, Dravidian texts of South India.
16 Alain Danielou, *Les Quatre Sens de la Vie* (Paris: Buchet/Chaste, 1984), p. 146.
17 Julius Evola, *The Metaphysics of Sex* (New York: Inner Traditions International, 1983).
18 Max Charlesworth et al (eds), *Religion in Aboriginal Australia*, (Queensland: University of Queensland Press, 1986), pp. 125–133.
19 Walker, *Tantrism*, p. 53.
20 Smith and de Simone, *Sex and the Brain*, p. 201.
21 Berman, *The Reenchantment of the World*.

Chapter 3: Toward a New Sexuality
22 Ashley Montague "Touching" extracts reprinted from Berman, *Reenchantment of the World*.
23 Batesman extract reprinted from Berman, *Reenchantment of the World*.
24 Phillip Aries extract reprinted from Berman, *Reenchantment of the World*.
25 Dr. Elmer Greene and Alice Greene, *Beyond Biofeedback* (New York: Delacorte, 1977), pp. 79–89.
26 Quote from Alain Danielou in conversation with Robert Lawlor.

Part 2: Sexuality and the Spiritual
1 Guy Murchie, *The Seven Mysteries of Life: An Exploration in Science and Philosophy* (Boston: Houghton Mifflin Company, 1978), p. 139.
2 Daniel Goleman, *Vital Lies, Simple Truths: The Psychology of Self Deception* (New York: Simon & Schuster, 1985), pp. 33–35.

Chapter 4: Symmetry and Sexuality
3 Alexander Wilder, *New Platonism and Alchemy* (Minneapolis: Wizards Bookshelf, 1975).
4 Julius Evola, *The Metaphysics of Sex* (New York: Inner Traditions International, 1983), pp. 150–160.
5 Robert Tonkinson, *The Marudjara Aborigines: Living the Dream in Australia's Desert* (Sydney: Holt, Rinehart and Winston, 1978).
6 Clyde E. Keeler, *Secrets of the Cuna Earthmother* (New York: Exposition Press, 1960), pp. 181–182.
7 *Sydney Morning Herald*, July 1988. Report on submissions given at an International Psychiatric Conference in Sydney that same month.

8 Weininger reference reprinted from Evola, *The Metaphysics of Sex.* Evola is deriving the qualities of the Absolute Feminine from a Taoist text translated by H. Maspero and presented in his article, "Les Procedes de 'nourir l'esprit vital' dans la religion taoiste ancienne," *Journal Asiatique* 229, April-June and July-September 1937, p. 158.

9 Margaret Courtney-Clarke, *Ndebelle: The Art of an African Tribe* (New York: Rizzoli, 1986), pp. 21–22.

10 *Brain/Mind Bulletin*, 2 June 1980.

11 Robert Ornstein, *Psychology of Consciousness* (San Francisco: Pelican Books, 1975), pp. 65–89.

12 *East West Journal*, August 1986.

13 Ernest Britt, *La Lyre d'Apollon* (Paris: Les Editions Vega, 1931), p. 87.

Chapter 5: Sex and History

14 Charlene Spretnak, "Knowing Gaia", *ReVision*, vol. 9, no. 2 Winter/Spring 1987 (Washington: Heldref Publications), pp. 69–73.

15 James Lovelock, *The Ages of Gaia* (New York: W.W. Norton and Co., 1988), pp. 3–14.

16 Spretnak, "Knowing Gaia", *ReVision*, pp. 69–73.

17 Alain Danielou, *Les Quatre Sens de la Vie* (Paris: Buchet/Chaste, 1984), p. 24.

18 Spretnak, "Knowing Gaia", *ReVision*, pp. 69–73.

19 Arthur M. Young, *The Geometry of Meaning* (San Francisco: Delacorte Press, 1976), p. 66.

Chapter 6: Sexuality in Philosophy, Religion and Myth

20 Ginette Paris, *Pagan Meditations* (Dallas: Spring Publications, 1988), p. 109.

21 Robert A. Johnson, *He: Understanding the Masculine Psychology* (New York: Harper & Row, 1986).

22 *New York Times*, May 1988.

23 Keeler, *Secrets of the Cuna*, p. 92.

24 Max Charlesworth et al (eds) *Religion in Aboriginal Australia* (Queensland: University of Queensland Press, 1986), pp. 125–133.

25 R.A. Schwaller de Lubicz, *Le Roi de la Theocratie Pharonique* (Paris: Flammarion, 1961), p. 163.

26 Keeler, *Secrets of the Cuna*.

27 Franklin Abbot (ed), *New Men, New Minds: Breaking Male Tradition* (California: The Crossing Press/Freedom, 1987), p. 166.

Chapter 7: Repression of the Feminine

28 Warren Farrell, *Why Men Are the Way They Are* (New York: McGraw-Hill, 1986), p. 244.

29 Linda Fierz-David, *Women's Dionysian Initiation* (Dallas: Spring Publications, 1988), pp. 72–78.

30 Peter Redgrove, *The Black Goddess and the Unseen Real* (New York: Grove Press, 1987), pp. 6–27.
31 Walter F. Otto, *Dionysus, Myth and Cult* (Texas: Spring Publications, 1981).
32 Edward C. Whitmont, *Return of the Goddess* (London: Routledge & Kegan Paul, 1982).

Otto, *Dionysus, Myth and Cult.*

C. Kerenyi, *Dionysos: Archetypal Image of Indestructible Life* (Princeton: Princeton University Press, 1975).
33 Whitmont, *Return of the Goddess*, pp. 54–57.
34 R. A. Schwaller de Lubicz, *Le Temple de l'Homme Caractères* 3, rue Hautefeville, Paris-6e, 1957.
35 Fierz-David, *Women's Dionysian Initiation*, p. 78.
36 Nancy Friday, *My Mother, My Self* (Glasgow: Collins/Fontana, 1977).

Chapter 8: Matriarchy: Reemergence of Female Sexuality
37 Whitmont, *Return of the Goddess*, pp. 11–23.
38 Alain Danielou, *Les Quatre Sens de la Vie* (Paris: Buchet/Chaste, 1984).
39 *Melbourne Herald*, 15 September 1988.
40 *Well Being Magazine*, Spring 1988 (Australian Edition).
41 *Time Magazine*, 29 February 1988.
42 Liz Greene, *Relating: An Astrological Guide to Living with Others on a Small Planet* (Kent: Coventure, 1984).

Part 3: Sexuality and Society
1 Max Charlesworth et al (eds) *Religion in Aboriginal Australia* (Queensland: University of Queensland Press, 1986), p. 57.

Chapter 9: Functions of Ritual
2 Liz Greene, *Relating: An Astrological Guide to Living with Others on a Small Planet* (Kent: Coventure, 1984).
3 Michel Beurdeley, *Chinese Erotic Art* (Fribourg: Chartwell Books Inc., 1969).
4 Allen Edwards and R.E.L. Masters, *Cradle of Erotica* (New York: Julian Press, 1965).
5 Ibid.
6 Dr. Stephen T. Chang, *The Tao of Sexology: The Book of Infinite Wisdom* (San Francisco: Tao Publishing, 1986).

Mantak Chia and Michael Winn, *Taoist Secrets of Love: Cultivating Male Sexual Energy* (New York: Aurora Press, 1986).

Mantak Chia and Maneewan Chia, *Healing Love Through the Tao: Cultivating Female Sexual Energy* (Huntington, N.Y.: 1986).

David A. Ramsdale and Ellen J. Dorfman, *Sexual Energy Ecstasy—*

A Guide to the Ultimate Intimate Sexual Experience (California: Peak Skill, 1985).

Chapter 10: Orgasm, Ritual, and Society
7 Ibid.
8 Chang, *The Tao of Sexology*, pp. 45–48.
9 Jo Durden-Smith and Diane de Simone, *Sex and the Brain* (London: Pan Books, 1983), pp. 212–214.
10 *Time Magazine*, 6 June 1988.
11 W. Edward Mann, *Orgone, Reich and Eros* (New York: Simon and Schuster, 1973).

Chapter 11: Patterns for a New Ritual Sexuality
12 Nik Douglas and Penny Slinger, *Sexual Secrets: The Alchemy of Ecstasy* (New York: Destiny Books, 1979).
13 Wendy D. O'Flaherty, *Asceticism and Eroticism in the Mythology of Sive* (Delhi: Oxford University Press, 1975).
14 Wilheim Reich, *Selected Writings: An Introduction to Orgonomy* (New York: Noonday Press, 1960), pp. 37–39.

Chapter 12: Another Threefold View of Sexuality
15 Robert A. Johnson, *He: Understanding the Masculine Psychology*, (New York: Harper & Row, 1986).
16 Ibid.
17 Chang, *The Tao of Sexology*.

Chia and Winn, *Taoist Secrets of Love.*

Chia and Chia, *Healing Love Through the Tao.*
18 Robert Lawlor, *Sacred Geometry, Philosophy, and Practice* (London: Thames and Hudson, 1987).
19 It is of interest to note that other Taoists such as Chia place the heart point approximately midway between the scrotum and the tip of the penis. Chang's system shows the position of the heart point on the male and female genitals each as an inverse reflection of one another, demonstrating the reciprocal harmonic concept underlying Taoist philosophy.
20 Chang, *The Tao of Sexology*, pp. 99–101; 183–184.
21 Ibid, pp. 199–200.

Chapter 13: Social Organization and Sexuality, Past and Future
22 Alain Danielou, *Les Quatre Sens de la Vie*, (Paris: Buchet/Chaste, 1984), pp. 119–125.
23 Edward C. Whitmont, *Return of the Goddess*, (London: Routledge & Kegan Paul, 1982), p. 121.
24 Danielou, *Les Quatre Sens de la Vie*, pp. 56–59.

Chapter 14: The Chemistry of Sexual and Social Reformation

25 Andrew Weil, M.D. and Winifred Rosen, Chocolates to Morphine, Understanding Mind-Active Drugs (Boston: Houghton Mifflin Co., 1983), pp. 81–84.

26 Andrew Weil, The Marriage of the Sun and Moon (Boston: Houghton Mifflin Co., 1980), pp. 249–251.

27 Weil and Rosen, Chocolates to Morphine, pp. 50–54.

28 Ibid.

29 Durk Pearson and Sandy Shaw, Life Extension (New York: Warner Book, 1982), pp. 120–121.

30 Richard A. Miller, The Magical and Ritual Use of Aphrodisiacs (New York: Destiny Books, 1985).

Chapter 15: Generation/Degeneration

31 The goddess Lakshmi from Hindu mythology exemplifies a fertility goddess who is transformed into the archetype of the female artist, temple dancer, poetess, and musician. A concluding story in the cycle of Lakshmi myths depicts the goddess emerging out of a lotus which sprang from the forehead of Vishnu (the forehead symbolizing the place of emergence into higher consciousness.) The lotus flower, some species of which send forth a flower directly from another below, is found as a symbol of spiritual rebirth and regeneration in Hindu and Egyptian mythology, and suggests a stage of development beyond procreative, earth-bound marriage and domesticity. Thus Lakshmi's evolution beyond the level of procreative fertility establishes a feminine model for woman as spiritual consort and temple courtesan. For further discussion see Sri Aurobindo, The Four Aspects of the Mother (Pondicherry, South India: Sri Aurobindo Ashram, 1969).

32 James Hillman, Loose Ends (Dallas: Spring Publications, 1983).

Chapter 16: Sexuality and the Universe Evolving

33 Robert Lawlor and Keith Critchlow, "Geometry and Architecture", Lindisfarne Letter #10 (Stockbridge: The Lindisfarne Press, 1980), pp. 60–65.

34 Charles Hampden Turner, Maps of the Mind, Charts and Concepts of the Mind and Its Labyrinths (London: Mitchell Beazley Publications, 1981).

35 John Moore, Sexuality Spirituality: A Study of Feminine/Masculine Relationships (London: Element Books, 1980).

Appendix

1 Alain Danielou, While the Gods Play (Rochester, Vt: Inner Traditions International, 1987), p. 96.

2 Clyde E. Keeler, Secrets of the Cuna Earthmother (New York: Exposition Press, 1960), p. 172.

SELECTED BIBLIOGRAPHY

Berman, Morris. *The Reenchantment of the World*. New York: Bantam Books, 1984.

Brauer, Alan P. and Brauer, Donna. *ESO (Extended Sexual Orgasm)*. Victoria: Horwitz Grahame, 1984.

Chang, Dr. Stephen T. *The Tao of Sexology: The Book of Infinite Wisdom*. San Francisco: Tao Publishing, 1986.

Chatwin, Bruce. *The Songlines*. London: Jonathan Cape, 1987.

Danielou, Alain. *While The Gods Play*. Vermont: Inner Traditions International, 1987.

Douglas, Nik and Slinger, Penny. *Sexual Secrets: The Alchemy of Ecstasy*. New York: Destiny Books, 1979.

Durden-Smith, Jo and de Simone, Diane. *Sex And The Brain*. London: Pan Books, 1983.

Easthope, Anthony. *What a Man's Gotta Do*. London: Paladin Grafton Books, 1986.

Evola, Julius. *The Metaphysics of Sex*. New York: Inner Traditions International, 1983.

Fierz-David, Linda. *Women's Dionysian Initiation*. Dallas: Spring Publications, 1988.

Issacs, Jennifer (ed). *Australian Dreaming*. Sydney: Lansdowne Press, 1987.

Keeler, Clyde E. *Secrets of the Cuna Earthmother*. New York: Exposition Press, 1960.

Krishnamurti, J. *The First and Last Freedom*, "Self Knowledge". New York: Harper & Row, 1975.

Liedloff, Jean. *The Continuum Concept*. Great Britain: Penguin, 1986.

Schwaller de Lubicz, R.A. *The Temple In Man*. Rochester, Vt.: Inner Traditions International, 1986.

Spencer, Sir W. Baldwin. *The Native Tribes of Central Australia*. London: Macmillan & Co., 1899.

Watts, Alan. *The Temple of Konarak: Erotic Spirituality.* London: Thames and Hudson, 1971.
Whitmont, Edward C. *Return Of The Goddess.* London: Routledge & Kegan Paul, 1982.

INDEX